Bor   London in 1939, Alan Ayckbour
chil   d in Sussex and was educated at Haileybury.
the: e Friday at the age of seventeen, he went into the thea
the   wing Monday and has been working in it ever since as
vari   y, a stage manager, sound technician, lighting technic
scen   inter, prop-maker, actor, writer and director. These
taler   leveloped thanks to his mentor, Stephen Joseph, who
he   net in 1958 upon joining the newly formed Library
T   in Scarborough. He was a BBC Radio Drama Produ
fr   65 to 1970, returning to Scarborough to take up the p
of .   ic Director of the Theatre in the Round, left vacant a
Ste   Joseph's death in 1967. Since that time, he has
pre   d over forty of his plays, first at the Library Theatre
fro   5 onwards, at the company's new converted base, th
Ste   Joseph Theatre. Some twenty-four of his plays have
sut   ntly been produced either in the West End or at the
Na   Theatre. They have been translated into forty langu
anc   been performed in virtually every continent of the
glo   ceiving many national and international awards in the
pro

TIME OF
MY LIFE
Alan Ayckbourn

faber and faber
LONDON · BOSTON

First published in 1993
by Faber and Faber Limited
3 Queen Square London WC1N 3AU

Photoset by Parker Typesetting Service, Leicester
Printed in England by Cox & Wyman Ltd, Reading, Berkshire

A CIP record for this book
is available from the British Library

ISBN 0–571–16990–2

2 4 6 8 10 9 7 5 3 1

CHARACTERS

GERRY, a businessman
LAURA, his wife
GLYN, their elder son
ADAM, their younger son
STEPHANIE, Glyn's wife
MAUREEN

CALVINU★, a restaurant owner
TUTO★, a head waiter
AGGI★, a waiter
DINKA★, another waiter
BENGIE★, yet another waiter

(★played by the same actor)

Scene: Calvinu's restaurant.
Time: Past, present and future.

Time of My Life was first performed in Scarborough at the Stephen Joseph Theatre in the Round on 21 April 1992. The cast was as follows:

GERRY STRATTON	Russell Dixon
LAURA	Colette O'Neill
GLYN	Richard Garnett
ADAM	Stephen Mapes
STEPHANIE	Karen Drury
MAUREEN	Sophie Heyman
CALVINU	Terence Booth
TUTO AGGI DINKA BENGIE	Terence Booth

Directed by	Alan Ayckbourn
Designed by	Roger Glossop
Lighting by	Mick Hughes

ACT ONE

The restaurant Essa de Calvi. It could be Greek, it could be Italian, even French or Spanish. It is none of these. It is whatever we decide to make it. It's a family concern, shabby but clean. Slightly under-lit. Distant piped music of indeterminate ethnic origins is heard from time to time.

There can be several tables on view depending on the space available. Only three need be used, though – two 'twos' set apart at a distance which are window tables and a large central table set for a party of six.

At the start there is a family dinner in progress at the main table. The other two are empty. The meal is all but over. It is around 10.30 pm on Saturday, 18 January.

Evidence of the supper litters the table. Used coffee cups, dirty plates, sweetpapers, full ashtrays and half-empty liqueur glasses. Also, evidence of gift wrapping paper, suggesting that someone has had a birthday.

At either end of the table sit the parents, LAURA *and* GERRY, *both in their fifties. He is a successful, self-made businessman. Originally a builder, he has diversified and managed to weather economic storms and recessions through a combination of astuteness and ruthlessness. There is no doubt that, visibly at least, he is very much the head of the family. A man who rarely if ever expects his words or actions to be questioned. But he hasn't achieved this single-handedly.* LAURA, *his wife, is also a force to be reckoned with, despite the fact that her profile, publicly, may suggest she exists purely to support her husband. But as so often in such partnerships, she has played a vital if largely unsung role in her husband's success. She is just as astute and every bit as determined.*

Thought they are both dressed for their evening out, GERRY *is more casually attired than his wife. Around and under Laura's chair are some of her birthday presents, now unwrapped. A large mantelpiece clock, a macramé flower basket holder and a slim volume of poems.* LAURA *is currently holding her other present, a pair of not unacceptable but modest 'craft' earrings.*

I

GERRY *and* LAURA *are a well-matched couple, and if their ambitions and drives have diminished slightly over the years and given way to a certain complacency and self-satisfaction, the pair are quite clearly, as they say, still on the board and in play – especially so far as their dealings with their own family are concerned.*

The closest of these, their two sons, GLYN *and* ADAM, *are also present.*

GLYN, *in his late twenties, is at first glance perhaps very much his father's son, a second version of his parent. But he has lived for too long in* GERRY's *shadow, has been compared unfavourably to his father just once too often, has tried to compete with an over-competitive parent and failed. He has been groomed to take over the family business, but it is unlikely that the firm will survive his father's death. He has charm but little of his father's drive or ambition.*

Across the table from him sits his wife, STEPHANIE. *In her mid-twenties, she has borne him one child and, as a result of recent emotional upheavals in her marriage, has worn less well than she should have done for someone reasonably comfortably off and with few material worries. One can only assume that in marrying* GLYN *she may have hoped she was marrying the father. She has since learnt better. Where she sought strength she has found weakness; instead of decisiveness nothing but vacillation and uncertainty.*

STEPHANIE *is seated next to her younger brother-in-law,* ADAM, *who is the apple of his mother's eye. In his early twenties, he is a nervous, uncoordinated windmill of a boy and in gatherings such as these hopelessly out of his depth.*

One of the reasons ADAM *is more anxious than usual tonight is due to the behaviour of his own partner seated across the table,* MAUREEN. *She is very much the outsider. She is Adam's new girlfriend and this is her first meeting with the family. She is very drunk. This has taken the form of a sort of glazed, fixed smiling trance. The room is evidently revolving for her quite rapidly, the floor rocking up and down at regular intervals. Whatever small contribution she might have made earlier to the evening is now reduced to a loud, regular hiccup. Apart from the occasional nervous glance from* ADAM, *the others have all chosen to act as if she doesn't exist.*

2

But now the party is nearly at an end. From a distance, a jolly group enjoying each other's company. After all, it is Laura's birthday and no one would want to spoil that.

Around the table, coffee pot in hand, flits TUTO, *one of several waiters we shall meet. They all have a marked resemblance – unsurprisingly, since they are all related in various ways to the head of the family and owner of the restaurant,* ERNESTO CALVINU. TUTO *is eternally cheerful and happy to serve.*

At the start, there are two conversations in progress, one between GERRY *and* GLYN *and another between* LAURA *and* STEPHANIE, *all talking across each other.* ADAM *and* MAUREEN *remain very much spectators.* LAURA *is holding a pair of earrings, evidently a present from* GLYN *and* STEPHANIE.

LAURA: (*To* STEPHANIE) . . . they're so unusual. That's what I love about them. I don't think I've seen anything like them before. Not even in Crete.

STEPHANIE: No, as I say, there's this woman we met at the nursery school, she's just started up. She's working from home but she was trained in jewellery making. She's fully trained. But she gave it up to have children but now they're at school she's just starting up again on her own from home . . .

LAURA: I've not seen anything like them anywhere. I think they're just lovely. I think I'll probably go to bed in them . . .

STEPHANIE: They suit you, I thought they'd suit you. They're your colour . . .

LAURA: They are. They're exactly my colour. I wear this colour all the time . . .

STEPHANIE: Yes, I've seen you wearing that colour . . . You've got that necklace that's not dissimilar, too, haven't you . . . You know, the one you sometimes wear with . . .

LAURA: Yes, I have. That's what I mean. I think they're the same stones. Semi-precious . . .

STEPHANIE: Semi-precious, yes . . .

LAURA: I prefer semi-precious, sometimes, you know. For certain occasions. I mean if you're just on your own, slopping around the house. You want to look good for

3

yourself but you don't necessarily want to look that special. I mean for that you want semi-precious, you don't necessarily want precious, do you?

STEPHANIE: No. I feel exactly the same. I know you're not supposed to . . .

LAURA: Well, a diamond. A beautiful diamond. That takes a lot of beating . . .

STEPHANIE: Oh well, a diamond . . . We're not talking about diamonds . . .

LAURA: And sapphires, I love sapphires. Gerry gave me a sapphire bracelet when we first moved to Forest Road . . .

STEPHANIE: I know, I've seen it on you. Oh, I covet that.

LAURA: Well, God knows what it cost him. A damn sight more than we could afford in those days. But I love it to death. I wear it a lot . . . it was the first bit of real jewellery I ever owned.

STEPHANIE: Yes . . .

LAURA: You know what I mean, real jewellery . . . ?

STEPHANIE: Yes, yes . . .

LAURA: I'd have worn it tonight, only . . .

STEPHANIE: I love that bracelet . . .

LAURA: I wear it a lot. Mind you, I'll wear these a lot, I think . . . I can see me wearing them a lot . . .

STEPHANIE: I'll give you her address . . .

LAURA: They're lovely . . . They'll do especially for daytime . . .

STEPHANIE: Well, they're meant for daytime, really . . . I'll let you have her address. She lives quite near us . . .

LAURA: Lovely, look at the light in them . . .

STEPHANIE: They look very good in daylight. They're daytime jewellery, really. But I think they're unusual, aren't they?

LAURA: They're certainly unusual . . .

STEPHANIE: All her stuff's unusual. She does shoe bags as well. I've got her card. I'll give it to you . . .

LAURA: Rubies. I quite like rubies, too. For certain occasions.

STEPHANIE: Yes. I'm not so sure about rubies.

(*Simultaneously with this*:)

GERRY: (*To* GLYN) . . . there's no use him complaining about deadlines and what should have been done then and what

4

wasn't done when it should have been done – he has to
understand we're talking today . . .

GLYN: Yes, yes, yes . . .

GERRY: . . . we're not talking twenty years ago when a supplier
was prepared to wait six, nine months – a year sometimes –
before he got paid.

GLYN: No, no . . .

GERRY: Most of the fellers we deal with nowadays, they're not
prepared to wait at all . . .

GLYN: No, no, no . . .

GERRY: . . . because they, in turn, have got cash-flow problems
just like anyone else.

GLYN: Yes, yes . . .

GERRY: . . . just as we have . . .

GLYN: Yes . . .

GERRY: . . . and they're not just reaching for things off shelves,
not these days . . .

GLYN: No, no . . .

GERRY: . . . they can't afford it any more than we can . . .

GLYN: No, no. Well, I said to him –

GERRY: . . . they're having to pay for them, cash up front . . .

GLYN: Yes, I explained to him . . .

GERRY: Those are the basic facts of life. He has to understand
them . . .

GLYN: Well I phoned him three times and –

GERRY: I mean, let's put it this way. What he's failing to
appreciate – what he is quite transparently failing to
appreciate – is the amount of *hidden* subsidy he's getting
from us – every time he withholds an account –

GLYN: Yes, I know, this is what I was –

GERRY: . . . that he has previously – let me finish – that he has
previously in writing and technically, legally bindingly –
agreed to pay . . .

GLYN: Well, it's easy to say that but . . .

GERRY: I'll talk to him. Don't worry, I'll talk to him tomorrow.
He's the same as his father, I knew his father and he used to
try it on. Eighteen months I had to wait for him, once . . .

GLYN: Yes, I know.

5

GERRY: Eighteen months and then he asked me, would I mind
overlooking the interest. I told him get – I told him . . .

GLYN: I know, I know . . .

GERRY: I mean, we were talking three or four hundred quid in
interest . . .

GLYN: Yes . . .

GERRY: That was a lot of money . . .

GLYN: It was . . .

GERRY: In those days . . .

GLYN: Quite.

GERRY: Times have changed, but it's still no different today –

GLYN: No.

GERRY: More brandy? Another brandy?

GLYN: No thanks, Dad, we need to be – Baby-sitter, you
know . . .

(During this, at some stage:)

ADAM:*(Softly, across to* MAUREEN*)* You alright?

*(*MAUREEN *nods miserably, but by way of a reply can only
hiccup. She is evidently feeling very sick.*

Meanwhile, simultaneously, TUTO *has been circling the table
offering fresh coffee.* STEPHANIE, MAUREEN, GLYN *and* ADAM
all decline when asked. LAURA *and* GERRY *both say yes.)*

TUTO: *(To* LAURA*)* More coffee? Madama? . . . Yes? Good.
Delicious coffee, with my own nuts. Yes? (To MAUREEN)
Madametta? More coffee? No? *(To* STEPHANIE*)* Madama?
Some lovely coffee? No? You break my heart. I cry all night.
(To GERRY*)* Mr Stratton? Yes? Yes. Of course. *(To* GLYN*)*
Seerar? No? No coffee? *(To* ADAM*)* Seerar? Of course.
Coffee. No? No coffee. Beautiful coffee. I grow it myself . . .
(Back to MAUREEN *whom he obviously fancies)* Madametta?
Please? No? Some liqueur? Crème de menthe? Some
Crouscac? Grown in my village, very rich, very sweet. Just
for the lady?

*(*MAUREEN *looks green.)*

No Crouscac? Some more sweet? Smooliboos? That is sugar
melted with rum and cream and baked with eggs in a
meringue case with a beautiful outside of chocolate and rich
fresh cream and glacé fruits. Delicious.

6

(MAUREEN's *stomach turns over.*)
Some trickletasse? This is delicious tart with treacle and
cream mixed with passion fruit, fresh strawberries and
armagnac . . .
(MAUREEN *rises suddenly from the table and makes a dash for
the door. This has the effect of stopping the other conversations.*)
Madametta . . . ?
ADAM: (*Rising, alarmed*) Maureen . . . (*Hastily, to the others*)
Excuse me . . .
(ADAM *goes out after* MAUREEN.)
TUTO: (*Slightly bemused*) Madametta, she is . . . ?
LAURA: (*Rather tight-lipped*) Madametta is slightly under the
weather, I'm afraid.
TUTO: Ah! I tell Seerar Calvinu . . .
(TUTO *goes off after them. A brief silence at the table.*)
LAURA: Oh dear, oh dear, oh dear . . .
GERRY: Yes . . .
LAURA: Where does he find them? Where does that boy find
them?
GERRY: (*Magnanimously*) Well . . .
LAURA: No, seriously, Gerry, there are dozens of girls who'd be
glad of him. Literally hundreds walking about out there.
They'd give their right legs for a boy like Adam . . .
STEPHANIE: It's not always that straightforward though, is
it . . . ?
LAURA: It's perfectly straightforward . . .
STEPHANIE: Not always . . .
LAURA: I'm sorry, I don't see the problem, I'm sorry.
STEPHANIE: It's meeting them, you have to get to meet them
first, don't you? I don't think Adam meets that many girls,
does he, Glyn?
GLYN: No, I don't think he meets that many . . .
LAURA: He could do if he wanted to – I don't care what they say,
even today it's still easier for a man. I mean Glyn met you,
didn't he?
STEPHANIE: Yes, he did . . .
LAURA: I mean Glyn's never had trouble meeting girls . . .
STEPHANIE: He hasn't . . .

7

LAURA: There we are, then. No, the trouble with Adam is they meet him. He doesn't have to look, they come out of the woodwork and seek him out, like that one did. He's a sitting target for every little tart in the district.

STEPHANIE: Now, I don't think that's very fair . . .

(TUTO *hurries through busily, he is calling another waiter, unseen.*)

TUTO: Bengie! Bengie! Chella bucketti. Ser madametta machosessa regorgettor. [*Bengie! Bengie! Fetch a bucket. The young lady has been sick in the gents.*] (*To the others*) It's OK. She's OK . . .

(TUTO *goes off in the other direction.*)

GERRY: Shouldn't someone see how she is?

LAURA: She's alright, Adam's with her . . .

GERRY: He's not going to be much use, is he? Not if she's bolted herself in the Ladies . . .

LAURA: She'll manage, it's her own fault. She was knocking them back like a goldfish . . . She had that champagne cocktail down in one gulp to start with, then she had three glasses of the Chablis . . .

GLYN: That was excellent . . .

GERRY: Yes, it was . . .

LAURA: . . . and at least four refills to my knowledge of that red I never touched . . .

GERRY: Australian that. Good, wasn't it?

GLYN: Australian? I thought it was Australian . . .

LAURA: And on top of that she had all that Benedictine, or whatever it was . . .

STEPHANIE: What were you doing, counting her?

LAURA: I couldn't help but noticing, could I? I'm surprised none of you did . . .

GERRY: We noticed . . .

LAURA: Not until it was too late, you didn't . . .

GERRY: Well . . .

LAURA: I say I don't know where he finds them.

GERRY: It's alright, it won't last. You know Adam . . .

STEPHANIE: It might. How do we know it won't?

LAURA: I hope to God it doesn't . . . I fear for that boy, sometimes.

8

GERRY: He's not a kid now, Laura. He's twenty-four years old
. . . It's his choice.
LAURA: He's twenty-three. He's not twenty-four till next
October. And I'm saying, it wasn't his choice –
GLYN: Twenty-three's a grown man . . .
LAURA: Maybe for you it was, for Adam at that age he's still
finding himself. And he needs protecting from girls like
that, who are just out for the main chance . . .
STEPHANIE: I think you're being really unfair to her, you
know . . .
GLYN: Nobody protected me from girls like that . . .
LAURA: Well, you. You both went into your marriage with your
eyes closed. Nothing I could do about that. You had to find
out for yourselves. Well, you've been through the tunnel,
you've both come out the other side, sadder but wiser and
with a bit of luck you've learnt your lesson, I hope, and
you'll know better next time. But with Adam, it's different.
He needs help, he can't cope with these things on his own.
He never could.
STEPHANIE: He's going to have to one day, isn't he?
LAURA: Not while I'm around. I'm amazed at you, Stephanie. I
thought as a mother yourself, you might understand how I
feel.
(STEPHANIE *holds back her reply.*
BENGIE, *a younger waiter who speaks no English, hurries
through anxiously.*)
BENGIE: (*Calling behind him*) . . . er goopini muckletracker, san?
[. . . *the mop in the cleaning cupboard, you say?*] (*To the others*)
'Scoos.
STEPHANIE: I think I'd better see if she needs some help.
LAURA: (*Rising*) No, it's alright, I'll go. I need to powder my
nose, anyway.
STEPHANIE: Let me know if I can –
LAURA: She'll be right as rain. She just needs her head in a
bucket . . . And quite frankly while we're at it, I do think a
son of mine can do a lot better for himself than a
hairdresser . . .
(LAURA *goes out.*)

9

GERRY: I don't think, somehow, that one's gone down too well with your mother.

STEPHANIE: She's fine. She was just very nervous, that's all . . .

GERRY: Nervous?

STEPHANIE: Not surprising, meeting you lot. I was nervous . . .

GLYN: What's wrong with being a hairdresser . . . ?

STEPHANIE: Nothing wrong with being a hairdresser . . .

GERRY: You know your mother . . .

STEPHANIE: I was a shop assistant, I'm amazed you let me through the front door . . .

GLYN: Ah well. It was only me you were marrying. Didn't matter so much, did it? And it was a very high-class shop, after all . . .

STEPHANIE: I only wish she'd leave Adam alone. He has to find out for himself, doesn't he?

GERRY: I've heard a rumour they're closing down, you know . . .

GLYN: What, Thackers?

STEPHANIE: Yes, I heard that too somewhere . . . Fancy. Established 1927.

GERRY: (*Gloomily*) Sign of the times. Sign of the times.

GLYN: By the way – do you think she liked the clock I gave her? Mother?

GERRY: She loved it. Did you not see her face when she opened it?

GLYN: Yes I did. I thought she seemed a bit – disapproving.

GERRY: She was over the moon with it.

GLYN: I can take it back and change it.

STEPHANIE: Don't bother. You did your best. You spent days choosing it. You never take that much trouble with my birthday.

GLYN: Well, you – generally know what you want, don't you . . . ?

(*Pause.* BENGIE *returns with a mop and bucket and hurries through.*)

GERRY: She's attractive, though. That girl. Good looker . . .

GLYN: Oh, yes . . .

STEPHANIE: Yes. (*Making to rise*) Well, we must be thinking of . . .

10

GERRY: Baby-sitters?

GLYN: Yes, right . . .

STEPHANIE: Otherwise we'll have to pay her for another two hours or something . . .

GLYN: Probably tucked up in our bed with her boyfriend by now . . .

STEPHANIE: (*Grimly*) She'd better not be . . .

GERRY: You bring the car?

GLYN: Oh, yes . . .

GERRY: You alright to drive?

STEPHANIE: Who do you think's driving? Muggins here.

GERRY: You're alright?

STEPHANIE: Of course.

GERRY: Only they've been tightening up . . .

STEPHANIE: I've had half a glass all evening. You know I never do . . .

GLYN: You hardly ate anything either . . .

STEPHANIE: What do you mean? I ate mountains.

GLYN: I was watching. Three mouthfuls and you pushed it away.

STEPHANIE: Well, I ate a lot for me . . . Anyway, I have to be careful. I start putting on weight, you're the first to complain.

GLYN: Never.

STEPHANIE: You do. A tub of lard in tights, he called me the other night . . .

GLYN: I did not, you called yourself that . . .

STEPHANIE: Well, maybe I did but I didn't want you going repeating it in the pub, did I? In front of everyone?

GERRY: You look lovely, Steph, you look a picture.

(GERRY *embraces* STEPHANIE *with mock passion*.)

STEPHANIE: Here's someone who appreciates me. (*Kissing* GERRY) That was a lovely meal, thank you, Gerry . . . As always.

GERRY: Well, it did cross my mind to take her somewhere else and then I thought, well . . . It's a tradition this place, isn't it? Every birthday, anniversary – we always seem to end up here. And it's your mother's favourite, so why not?

GLYN: We've been using it a bit lately. From the office. It's quite convenient. Have you ever tried lunch here?

GERRY: No, never lunch . . .

GLYN: Very good. Reasonable prices, too , aren't they?

STEPHANIE: Don't ask me. You never take me out to lunch.

GLYN: I would do, I would do. You've only to ask . . .

GERRY: I'd take him up on that, Steph.

STEPHANIE: I will, don't worry.

GERRY: I'll see you to the door . . .

STEPHANIE: There's no need.

GERRY: No, I'll get the bill at the same time – (*Stopping them*) Listen, just before we . . . Steph. Glyn.

GLYN: Yes.

GERRY: I hope you appreciate, this business with you two – getting together again – patching it up between you – it couldn't have been a better birthday present for her, I'm telling you.

STEPHANIE: (*Not wishing to prolong this*) Well, maybe . . .

GERRY: No, Steph, I don't think you properly – I mean Glyn and I, we know her – and sometimes she comes over, you know, as maybe a bit blunt, plain spoken, you know. Even tough, sometimes, yes. Well, yes, Laura can be tough. But underneath all that, she's a very vulnerable woman. A very caring person and someone who gets hurt quite easily.

STEPHANIE: Yes, I'm sure.

GERRY: Now you two, you've had your moments – you and her, Steph. I know you have. You've had your disagreements – but let's say, starting today, it's a new leaf, alright? A new leaf for you and her, Steph. And a new leaf for you two. Right.

GLYN: Dead right. (*He puts his arm around* STEPHANIE. STEPHANIE *stands rather awkwardly.*)

GERRY: You see, if anything happened to – Well, you know how we both care for Timmy, don't you?

STEPHANIE: Oh, yes.

GERRY: Laura'a always – I think she's always secretly dreamt of grandchildren – I think she wanted grandchildren more than she wanted children . . .

STEPHANIE: Difficult . . .

GLYN: Oh, yes, she's always wanted them, I think . . . I mean she's never said it in so many words, but —

STEPHANIE: Well, she's got one . . .

GERRY: Yes, but when we thought, you know, you and Glyn
were all washed up, I mean . . . Maybe not get to see
Stephanie — and Timmy again . . .

STEPHANIE: (*Slightly impatiently*) Yes, we're back together now
though, aren't we?

GERRY: (*Kissing her again*) Yes, you are! You are! (*To* GLYN)
And he's going to behave himself from now on, aren't you?

GLYN: It's all in the past, Dad.

GERRY: Send her packing. Do you hear?

GLYN: I've sent her packing.

GERRY: We used to have a word for women like that . . .

GLYN: Yes, OK . . .

GERRY: Not a very pleasant word . . .

STEPHANIE: Sorry, Gerry, we really must go . . .

GERRY: (*Ignoring her*) No more, do you hear? No more.

GLYN: No more, promise.

GERRY: Word of honour?

GLYN: Word of honour, Dad.

GERRY: (*Grasping* STEPHANIE *again*) You stand by this one, you
hear me? You stand by this lovely girl or you'll have me to
answer to next time . . .

(ADAM *returns rather anxiously.*)

STEPHANIE: How is she?

ADAM: She's alright, she's —

GLYN: Does she need a lift anywhere . . . ?

ADAM: No, she's fine. I'll see her home. She just needs her
handbag . . .

STEPHANIE: Has she been sick?

ADAM: Yes.

STEPHANIE: Best thing.

ADAM: In the Gents.

GERRY: The Gents?

ADAM: Yes.

GERRY: Bloody hell, Adam.

ADAM: She was in that much of a hurry she misread the
signs . . .

GERRY: There's a bright pink door and a bright blue door, what else does she need?

ADAM: Well, she wasn't feeling too good . . .

GERRY: All the women in the world and you have to take up with a colour-blind hairdresser. I don't know . . . Is she still in there?

ADAM: No, she's in the Ladies now . . .

GERRY: Just as well. I want to use the other one . . .

ADAM: I'll just get her bag. Take her home.

GERRY: (*As he goes*) Bloody hell, I don't know. It's your mother's birthday, son.

(GERRY *goes out*.)

ADAM: Sorry.

STEPHANIE: Take her home. She'll be alright. Probably have a bit of a hangover, that's all.

ADAM: I don't know why she – She doesn't drink, you see. Normally. Hardly at all.

STEPHANIE: I was saying, she was probably nervous.

ADAM: Yes, she was. I mean, I told her there was no need to be but –

GLYN: Never mind. You know what they say about buses. There'll be another along in a minute. Same with women . . .

STEPHANIE: Oh shut up, that's fat lot of help, isn't it . . .

GLYN: Plenty more fish . . .

ADAM: It's not as simple as that. The trouble is – I'm in love with her –

GLYN: (*Laughing*) Oh, great . . .

ADAM: I am.

GLYN: Has there ever been one you haven't been in love with?

ADAM: Not like this. Never like this.

STEPHANIE: She's certainly in love with you . . .

ADAM: You think so? How do you know?

STEPHANIE: Because I was looking at her –

ADAM: You could tell by looking at her?

STEPHANIE: Of course. It was obvious. She couldn't take her eyes off you.

GLYN: What do you mean? She was touching me up under the table for half the meal.

ADAM: She was not!

STEPHANIE: She certainly wasn't. Or I'd have cut her fingers off.

ADAM: You really think she loves me?

STEPHANIE: I keep saying. Hasn't she told you?

ADAM: Yes, but . . .

STEPHANIE: Then she most probably means it. (*Pleasantly to* GLYN) Some people do . . .

(LAURA *returns.*)

LAURA: (*With some satisfaction*) Well, she looks a right mess now, I must say. I doubt if they'll let her in here again in a hurry.

ADAM: I must take her bag to her. Is she alright?

LAURA: As far as I know. I left her in there, washing her face. (*To* GLYN *and* STEPHANIE) She was sick in the Gents, you know. Not even the Ladies.

STEPHANIE: Yes, we heard.

(ADAM *starts a hunt for Maureen's handbag.*)

LAURA: There's a great queue of men waiting to get in while they clean up.

STEPHANIE: Oh, dear.

LAURA: Including your father.

STEPHANIE: Oh, well. Goodnight, Laura.

LAURA: Oh, are you both off? Goodnight, then.

(LAURA *and* STEPHANIE *kiss quite sedately.*)

And thank you for the lovely present, Steph. As I say, I'll wear them all the time. Goodnight, Glyn. And thank you for the clock . . .

GLYN: (*Anxiously*) It was what you wanted, was it? You really liked it?

ADAM: (*Having located the bag under the table*) Excuse me . . .

LAURA: Just a minute, Adam . . .

ADAM: I just have to . . .

LAURA: Just a quick word. (*Embracing* GLYN, *rather peremptorily*) Goodnight, dear.

GLYN: 'Night, Mum. See you Thursday.

LAURA: Thursday?

GLYN: We're bringing Timmy up to visit you, aren't we?

LAURA: (*Unenthusiastically*) Oh yes, lovely.

STEPHANIE: Goodnight, Adam. And remember what I told you.

ADAM: Oh, yes. Right. 'Night.

GLYN: 'Night, Ad. (*As they go, to an unseen waiter*) Thank you. That was lovely.

STEPHANIE: (*Likewise*) Yes, lovely, yes. Thank you.

(STEPHANIE *and* GLYN *go out.*)

LAURA: What's she been telling you, then?

ADAM: Who?

LAURA: Stephanie. What was it she told you?

ADAM: (*Evasively*) Oh, nothing. I forget.

LAURA: Well. I think you know what I'm going to say, don't you?

ADAM: Yes.

LAURA: Do I need to say it?

ADAM: No. You don't like her. She's not right for me. She's common. She ate her melon with the wrong knife, I don't know . . .

LAURA: Now, come on, be sensible . . .

ADAM: She wears her shoes on the wrong feet . . .

LAURA: Now I'm not like that, you know that. I'm not. You know you're free to choose. You're perfectly free. You're twenty-four years old in October and you're old enough by now to make your own mistakes.

ADAM: Then I will.

LAURA: All I'm saying is, we both care for you. You know that. We care for you more than anything in the world. So you have to see we both can't just stand by and say nothing at all. What sort of people would we be if we did that?

ADAM: Yes, I realize that what you're saying you feel is for the –

LAURA: If we stood there watching you throw your life away?

ADAM: I'm not throwing my life away . . .

LAURA: Adam, she's an alcoholic . . .

ADAM: She's not an alcoholic . . .

LAURA: Adam, darling, I've seen alcoholics. I've lived with them. Your own father's brother, your Uncle David, he was an alcoholic. Please don't try to teach me about alcoholics, Adam. Please. I'm telling you, that girl is a virtual alcoholic.

ADAM: Mum, it was only tonight. She was nervous. She never drinks normally.

LAURA: No, Adam, listen. Listen to what you're saying. What

you're saying is, you've never normally caught her
drinking . . .

ADAM: I'd know if she drank. I'd know.

LAURA: How could you know? How? You're not trained . . .

ADAM: Well, I'm close to her. I kiss her and – things . . .

LAURA: Oh, don't worry. There's ways. They have ways. Your
Uncle David used to suck mothballs. Just to cover the
smell . . .

ADAM: No wonder he died.

LAURA: He died of drink, Adam. Drink. With a liver the size of
Wembley Stadium. After we'd all nursed him for two years.
Watching him die. You want to finish up doing that?

ADAM: On come on, this is ridiculous. Maureen's not –

LAURA: Maureen's a young woman with a serious personal
problem and a shrewed eye for the main chance . . .

ADAM: I'm not listening to this –

LAURA: Adam . . .

ADAM: I'm not. I'm sorry.

LAURA: Adam, do you want to break your father's heart? Because
that's what you're going to end up doing . . .

ADAM: Oh, bollocks . . .

LAURA: You want to kill your own father, go ahead . . .

ADAM: Oh, bugger off!

(ADAM *storms off, passing* TUTO.)

TUTO: Goodnight, seerar. Everything satisfactory? Good. We try
to please. Madama Stratton, sooe more coffee?

LAUWA; (*Tight-lipped*) Yes, I think I need some, Tuto. Thank
you very much.

TUTO: Cer – tainly! (*He makes to go.*)

LAURA: And I'll have a large Rémy Martin as well, please.

TUTO: Large Rémy – cer – tainly.

(TUTO *goes off cheerfully.* LAURA *sits down again at the table.*
GERRY *returns.*)

GERRY: Right then. I've asked for the bill.

LAURA: He just swore at me.

GERRY: Who did? The waiter?

LAURA: No. Adam. He's just sworn at me. Told me to B–U–G–
off.

GERRY: (*Shrugging*) Well . . .

LAURA: No, not 'well'. He shouldn't use language like that. Not to his mother. That's not how we brought him up. You'd have walloped him at one time.

GERRY: I never walloped him, you wouldn't let me. It was Glyn I walloped . . .

LAURA: Fat lot of good that did . . .

GERRY: Anyway. He's upset. She's embarrassed him. He's upset. He's made a mistake. He realizes that.

LAURA: Well, I only hope he does . . . He seems very stuck on her.

GERRY: He's only got to take one look at her now. Enough to put him off for life. By God she looks a mess. All down her –

LAURA: Yes, I know . . .

GERRY: All over her dress and shoes. All down her tights.

LAURA: Yes, I know, I saw her. You don't have to go into details . . .

GERRY: Dear, oh dear. Ruined her dress.

LAURA: I've no sympathy.

(BENGIE *returns with the brandy*.)

Thank you.

GERRY: What's that you're having?

LAURA: A brandy.

GERRY: Another one?

LAURA: I needed it.

GERRY: Well, in that case I'll join you . . . (*To* BENGIE) Oy! I say! I say! I'll have a brandy as well –

(BENGIE *shakes his head, not comprehending*.)

A brandy. One brandy.

LAURA: He doesn't speak English. Why can't they find waiters that speak English?

GERRY: Bran-deee. (*To* LAURA) They're all relations of Calvinu's. He has them shipped over in packing cases.

BENGIE: (*Recognizing a word*) Calvinu! Mente! [*One moment*.]

(BENGIE *hurries out*.)

GERRY: Get some nice presents, did you?

LAURA: Well, apart from yours, which is lovely, thank you very much – I got some earrings from Stephanie, which I must say

for once I might actually wear occasionally. I've got drawers
full of stuff she's given me, I never touch. You think she'd
have noticed by now. Never known a woman with so many
friends that make cheap jewellery. That or home-made
pottery. Glyn? Glyn gave me that damn great clock I certainly
don't want and I've no idea where to put. Adam gave me a
lovely little book of poetry which he wrote in, which was nice.
He knows I like poetry. Well, some poetry. As for that girl, I
can't work out what she's given me at all. A piece of knotted
string as far as I can see. (*She holds up the object in question.*)

GLYN: (*Considering it*) Well . . .

LAURA: I mean, what is it? You tell me . . .

GERRY: Hang on, I know. It's one of those hanging things. For
hanging things in. Pots.

LAURA: Pots?

GERRY: For flowers. Flower pots. Hanging baskets. Probably
made it herself.

LAURA: (*Tossing the item aside*) Yes, I should think she probably did
from the look of it.
(*TUTO returns with a pot of coffee.*)

TUTO: More coffee? Delicious coffee.

LAURA: Thank you.

TUTO: Bengie bring you the brandy?

LAURA: Yes. We want another one, please.

TUTO: One more brandy. Rémy Martin, yes?

GERRY: That'll do.

TUTO: Seerar, more coffee?

GERRY: Thank you.

TUTO: (*Calling off*) Hey, Bengie, ennesta gap ay Rémy Martin..
[Another glass of Rémy Martin.] Rémy Martin! (*Shaking his
head*) Yey yey yey. He's very young.

LAURA: Yes?

TUTO: He's also a little stupid.

GERRY: Oh yes?

TUTO: Very, very stupid. Otherwise why does he come over here,
eh?
(*TUTO goes off laughing. GERRY and LAURA look slightly
dubious.*)

GERRY: Well, at least they're back together. Glyn and Steph.
That's the main thing.

LAURA: How long for though . . . ?

GERRY: Oh, I think they'll make a go of it, this time. He's had his
fling . . .

LAURA: I know Glyn was largely to blame – I'm sure he'd drive any
woman up the wall – but frankly I do think you'd have to be
some sort of a saint to live with that girl for any length of
time . . .

GERRY: Stephanie?

LAURA: I mean, she's not an easy person.

GERRY: Oh, I get on with her. I like her.

LAURA: You would, you're a man. She makes the effort for you.
But I've seen her on her own. And I'll tell you this,
underneath she is self-centred and selfish.

GERRY: I won't hear a word against her . . .

LAURA: I tell you she leads Glyn a dance. It's not all one way.

GERRY: How do you mean? You mean she's having an affair?

LAURA: No, I'm not saying that. She wouldn't have the nous. But
you don't have to climb into bed with people to lead them a
dance, do you?

GERRY: I don't know what you're talking about.

LAURA: You wouldn't, you're a man.

(BENGIE *returns with a brandy*.)

BENGIE: Rémy Martin?

GERRY: Yes, over here. Thank you.

BENGIE: Rémy Martin.

GERRY: Thank you.

BENGIE: Rémy Martin. Thank you.

(BENGIE *goes out*.)

GERRY: Cheers.

LAURA: Good health.

(*They drink*.)

What'll happen to Adam, do you think? What'll become of him?

GERRY: No idea, he's like you. I've never understood him, either.

LAURA: He is. He's exactly like me. He's a worrier. That's what
worries me. He ought to be settled. He ought to have found
himself a career by now. A proper career. A proper woman.

20

GERRY: Well, haven't I offered him a job with us? A decent job. Not a sinecure, maybe, but a safe job with the firm. Like Glyn has. Not Glyn's responsibilities, perhaps, but then Glyn's that bit more responsible, but still a responsible job, challenging.

LAURA: He's destined for better things than that . . .

GERRY: (*Indignant*) What do you mean, better things?

LAURA: Just sitting behind a desk all day. That's maybe alright for Glyn . . .

GERRY: He doesn't just sit behind a desk all day, what do you think we do . . . ?

LAURA: . . . but then Glyn's got the imagination of a coat hanger . . .

GERRY: The job I offered Adam had good money, good prospects. Not a desk job either. Not at all. Using his brain, getting out and about. Meeting different people. There's a lot would be glad of that. But he'd rather waste his time with his poetry magazines and what have you . . .

LAURA: That's not wasting time . . .

GERRY: He's got a genius for timing, that boy. Four hundred businesses going to the wall every week, three million unemployed, world recession, God knows what else and he decides to start a bloody poetry magazine. I mean he's a nice enough lad and he's your son but in my opinion he's a couple of sandwiches short of a picnic, that one.

LAURA: *Our* son. He's *our* son. And it's an arts magazine. It covers all the arts. Locally.

GERRY: (*Uninterested*) Does it? Single sheet, is it?

LAURA: He left you a copy only you never even looked at it.

GERRY: I mean, we're feeling the pinch badly enough. And we're at the top end of the market, we are.

LAURA: (*Suddenly alert*) We're not in trouble, are we?

GERRY: No. Not yet. If things go on as they are much longer we might be. But not yet.

LAURA: My God. I'd no idea. You never talk to me about these things . . .

GERRY: There's no point, is there? You're not interested.

LAURA: I'm certainly interested if we're going broke –

GERRY: We're not going broke . . .

LAURA: You just said –

GERRY: Keep your voice down. I said we might be if. That's all. If. Things go on as they are. That's all I said. But they probably won't do, so forget I said it. Forget all about it. Shut up about it, altogether. It's your birthday, for God's sake.

(*Pause.*)

LAURA: I never realized we were in trouble . . .

(*The lights dim slightly on* GERRY *and* LAURA, *who continue to sit silently sipping their brandies, both lost in their own thoughts.*

They will continue in 'present' time. That is to say, the rest of the play, as far as they are concerned, is the remainder of their evening together – approximately two hours. For the other characters, time behaves somewhat differently. For STEPHANIE *and* GLYN, *who are shortly to enter, theirs is 'future' time which will stretch ahead over a period of two years.*

The lights now come up on one of the corner tables for two. It is lunchtime on Friday, 24 January, almost a week later. It is raining hard outside.

A waiter, DINKA, *a rather sour man in his thirties, enters, leading* STEPHANIE *to the table. Despite the rain she has obviously made some effort with her appearance this morning.*)

DINKA: (*Without ceremony*) Here, this one here.

STEPHANIE: (*Rather breathless from running*) Thank you.

DINKA: It's all we got.

STEPHANIE: It's fine. Can I get rid of my – ? (*Indicating her wet coat.*)

(DINKA *holds out his hand without offering to help.*)

(*Struggling out of her coat*) Terrible downpour. Just got caught in it. Of course I had to park miles away . . . you know . . .

(*Handing* DINKA *her coat*) Thank you.

DINKA: It's for one?

STEPHANIE: No, I said there's two of us, my husband should be here any – (*seeing him*) Oh yes, there he is. (*Calling*) Glyn! (*To* DINKA) Don't go away, he may want to order a drink.

DINKA: You want a drink?

STEPHANIE: No, I don't want one. My husband might want a drink. I'll just have some water, please.

22

DINKA: You want water?

STEPHANIE: Yes, some still water. Not fizzy . . .

(GLYN *enters. Unlike Stephanie's, his clothes are hardly wet at all.*)

GLYN: Sorry . . . One drop of rain, every bit of traffic grinds to a halt.

STEPHANIE: You didn't drive here . . . ?

GLYN: I wasn't getting drowned.

STEPHANIE: You're only just round the corner. It's a two-minute walk.

GLYN: I'm not walking, not in this.

STEPHANIE: Did you get parked?

GLYN: Yes, just outside.

STEPHANIE: God, some people. I'm way over in Pond Street.

DINKA: You want a drink?

GLYN: Yes, I'll have a Scotch with water. You want something?

DINKA: Scotch with water.

GLYN: You having something?

STEPHANIE: Yes, just water.

DINKA: Fizzy water?

STEPHANIE: No, plain water, please.

DINKA: (*Moving away*) Plain water.

GLYN: (*After* DINKA) And we'll have some menus at the same time. We're in a hurry.

DINKA: Menus.

(DINKA *goes off.*)

GLYN: I see we've got Cheerful Charlie.

STEPHANIE: Is it usually this busy in here at lunchtimes?

GLYN: Generally. So. How is she?

STEPHANIE: Well, I was there for about an hour with her. And she was sitting up the whole time. She's still on drugs, of course, but she seems much brighter than she was. You know talking and answering. Following what you're saying.

GLYN: How's the bruising? Has that gone down?

STEPHANIE: Yes. Well, it's still there of course – but her face is nearly back to normal. She doesn't look anything like as bad as she did.

GLYN: How is she in herself . . . ?

23

STEPHANIE: Well, alright. As well as you can expect – it's going to take some time, Glyn . . . They were very close, weren't they?

GLYN: There were. Inseparable.

STEPHANIE: I don't think she's properly taken it in, really.

GLYN: Did she mention him . . . ? Did she ask about Dad?

STEPHANIE: No. Not at all. Not once.

GLYN: At least she's sitting up and taking notice.

STEPHANIE: Yes, she is. Well, as much notice as she ever takes of me, which isn't a lot. She never enjoys talking to me. She wanted you there really. Or Adam, of course, ideally . . .

GLYN: (*Anxiously*) I hope you explained I was – I mean I'll be up there, first thing this evening –

STEPHANIE: I told her you were busy –

GLYN: You bet I was busy. But I can be there from this evening. All night, if necessary . . .

STEPHANIE: You won't need to do that. She's being nursed. She's sedated. She'll be sleeping, anyway. Listen, how are things? At work?

GLYN: Chaos. The trouble with Dad was, he wouldn't delegate. When he died, half the secrets died with him. Where the hell's Adam, then? Why hasn't he been up to see her? He hasn't got anything else to do.

STEPHANIE: They said he looked in yesterday morning. He was there about ten minutes and fainted.

GLYN: Fainted?

STEPHANIE: Apparently.

GLYN: What was the matter with him?

STEPHANIE: Nothing. Just hospitals, I think.

GLYN: Typical.

STEPHANIE: He brought that Maureen along with him. That didn't help. You know how your mother feels about Maureen.

GLYN: What did she do this time, throw up all over the bed?

STEPHANIE: No, she's not like that, not at all. She's a nice kid. She brought your mother some paper flowers.

GLYN: Paper flowers?

STEPHANIE: Yes, she'd made them herself. Out of tissue paper.

They were beautiful. She's ever so clever with her hands.

GLYN: Did Mother appreciate them?

STEPHANIE: Oh, you know her, she chucked them in the bin soon as they'd left. I picked them out, though, and brought them home . . .

GLYN: (*Looking around, impatiently*) Where's this man gone to? I want to order.

STEPHANIE: . . . they look lovely in that alcove above the telly.

GLYN: I've got meeting after meeting this afternoon. You've no idea.

STEPHANIE: Will you be home late again?

GLYN: Probably. I'll pop up and see Mother, of course. I may have to come back. Sorry.

STEPHANIE: No. Thanks for finding time for lunch. Haven't seen you for days, have I?

GLYN: Won't last for ever. Back to normal soon.

STEPHANIE: I hope so. I miss you. So does Timmy.

GLYN: I miss you.

STEPHANIE: Do you? Really?

GLYN: Of course.

STEPHANIE: You really miss us? You're not just saying that?

GLYN: Of course not. I wouldn't say it if I didn't mean it, would I?

STEPHANIE: You might.

GLYN: Why should I? Why should I do that?

STEPHANIE: Well – to keep me quiet.

GLYN: You think I'd do that?

STEPHANIE: You have done in the past, haven't you? Said you loved me when you were –

GLYN: Now, that's in the past. Well in the past. Alright? That's forgotten. We agreed. Alright?

STEPHANIE: Yes.

GLYN: I gave you my word, didn't I?

STEPHANIE: Yes.

GLYN: I promised you. And I promised – (*He breaks off.*)

STEPHANIE: You promised who?

GLYN: I promised Mum and Dad.

STEPHANIE: You promised them?

GLYN: Yes.

STEPHANIE: When? When did you do that?

GLYN: Oh, last Saturday evening, when we were all together . . . on her birthday, you know.

STEPHANIE: Why?

GLYN: Why what?

STEPHANIE: Why did you promise them? What's it to do with them?

GLYN: It's everything to do with them. I'm their son for one thing.

STEPHANIE: It's our marriage . . .

GLYN: Yes, and they – they were anxious that it succeeded.

STEPHANIE: Why?

GLYN: Because they wanted us to be happy. That's natural, isn't it?

STEPHANIE: But we weren't happy, were we?

GLYN: No, maybe we weren't then. But we are now, aren't we?

STEPHANIE: Yes, we are now. But they weren't to know we would be, were they? When you left me and went off to live with *her* that was because you were no longer happy with me, wasn't it? You were happier with *her*, weren't you? So if they'd had your happiness at heart they'd have suggested you stayed with *her*, wouldn't they? Instead of coming back to me?

GLYN: I came back to you because I wanted to come back to you . . . Me. I decided it. Nobody else. Me. Alright?

STEPHANIE: Then why did you need to make promises to them?

GLYN: Just to keep them happy, that's all . . .

STEPHANIE: I see. Did you promise *her* anything? Just to keep *her* happy?

GLYN: No, I did not. Don't be stupid.

STEPHANIE: I just wondered.

GLYN: She's got a name you know. *Her*. She's got a name.

STEPHANIE: I prefer *her*.

GLYN: Fair enough.

(*Slight pause*.)

STEPHANIE: We are happy, aren't we?

GLYN: Yes. We're happy. I think we're happy. Aren't we? Pretty

happy, anyway. Who the hell ever knows when they're
happy? I don't know.

(*At this point, the owner of the restaurant,* ERNESTO CALVINU,
*enters. An ample man in late middle age. He carries a tray on
which is the whisky, a small jug of water, a bottle of carbonated
water and an extra glass. Under his arm are two menus.*)

Ah, Ernesto!

CALVINU: Mr Stratton. What can I say? I am so, so sorry. I am
devastated. We are all devastated. In the kitchen. All the
waiters, the cashier, the hat check girl. Such a loss. Such a
loss . . .

GLYN: It is. It is.

CALVINU: When we heard, we couldn't believe – the same Mr
Stratton? My friend Gerry who was in here all these years?
Unbelievable.

GLYN: Yes, it is. Unbelievable.

CALVINU: Unbelievable.

GLYN: Darling, you know Ernesto, don't you – Ernesto Calvinu?

STEPHANIE: Yes, of course, we've . . .

CALVINU: Of course, of course. Only the other might. Madama,
please excuse me. This news has made me – all over the place –

STEPHANIE: Of course.

CALVINU: Gerry Stratton and I. We were old friends. Only the
other night you were all here. Your poor mother . . . Poor
Laura.

GLYN: Yes . . .

CALVINU: It was the same night? The car?

GLYN: Yes. He was driving home from here with my mother . . .

CALVINU: Your mother . . .

GLYN: . . . and they – just came off the road . . .

CALVINU: . . . . off the road . . .

GLYN: . . . no other vehicle . . .

CALVINU: . . . no vehicle, no . . .

GLYN: . . . and – it's a mystery.

CALVINU: It's a mystery. It's a mystery. It's a mystery.

GLYN: Yes.

CALVINU: Mystery, hmm?

GLYN: Yes.

27

CALVINU: But your mother? She's alright?

GLYN: She's –

STEPHANIE: She'll be fine.

CALVINU: Excuse me. Your drinks. Scotch and water.

GLYN: Thank you.

CALVINU: Fizzy water for the lady.

STEPHANIE: Oh, I really wanted –

CALVINU: Please. On the house. On the house.

GLYN: Thank you.

STEPHANIE: Thank you.

CALVINU: Please. The menus. Madama, Seerar.

STEPHANIE: Thank you.

GLYN: Thank you.

CALVINU: The special today is vissviss. That is minced beef cooked very, very rare and served on red cabbage with a sauce of fresh beetroot. (*Looking at them.*) Maybe not today, though? 'Scoos. I will leave you in peace.

GLYN: Thank you.

STEPHANIE: Thank you.

> (CALVINU *departs. A silence.*)

GLYN: Nice man. Well, what are you going to have then?

> (*The lights dim on them and we return to* GERRY *and* LAURA *at the main table. They are seated as before, still sipping their brandy. It is, in their time scale, a few moments later.*)

LAURA: I mean, if we're going bankrupt I think I should be told about it, don't you?

GERRY: (*Irritably*) We're not going bankrupt. Who said we were going bankrupt?

LAURA: That's what you seemed to be hinting at just now.

GERRY: We're a long way from being bankrupt. A long way. We just have – one or two cash-flow problems, that's all. Actually, if you must know, they're not our problems at all. They're other people's problems. Only they get passed on. Their problem becomes your problem, that's all.

LAURA: So there is a problem, then?

GERRY: Yes, there's a problem. There's a problem. But it's solvable. They always are, problems. That's what they're put there for.

LAURA: What do you do to solve it? I mean, if you're running out of money how do you solve it?

GERRY: You use your imagination, don't you? Make creative use of what you've got.

LAURA: Creative? What's creative?

GERRY: You know, like that son of yours gets . . .

LAURA: I presume you're referring to Adam?

GERRY: He's the only creative one round here, isn't he? He's our poet.

LAURA: He's not a poet.

GERRY: Oh, I beg his pardon. I thought that's what he was this week.

LAURA: He edits a magazine. If you read it, you'd know . . .

GERRY: Pop video maker, entrepreneur – whatever that is – documentary film director – television cameraman – he was going to be one of them for a bit, wasn't he? And what happened to that theatre he was going to open? Haven't heard much about that lately either, have we?

LAURA: Leave him alone. He doesn't bother you. He never asks you for money, does he?

GERRY: No, he doesn't. He asks you and that's worse.

LAURA: I can do what I like with my money.

GERRY: And who gives you that money in the first place, may I ask?

LAURA: You do.

GERRY: Precisely.

LAURA: And I earn every bloody penny of it, so don't you start that one.
(*Pause.*)

GERRY: (*Suddenly bad tempered*) I want another brandy.

LAURA: It's gone half past eleven –

GERRY: Who cares, I want another brandy. (*Calling*) Hey! Hey, waiter! (*Rising*) Oh, what the hell, I'll get it myself, it's quicker.
(*He rises.*)

LAURA: He'll be back in a minute, he's busy.

GERRY: I need the Gents as well. Hopefully they'll have cleaned it up by now.

29

(*He goes out.*)

LAURA: (*After him*) Don't order anything for me, will you . . .

(*The lights fade on them and come up on* ADAM *and* MAUREEN, *who have apparently just finished a meal together. Their time is 'past' time. From their viewpoint we are now one week prior to the birthday supper, on an evening earlier that same month, Saturday, 11 January. We will follow them gradually further back in time over a period of two months to the point where they first met.*

MAUREEN *is sitting miserably, playing with objects on the table, fidgety and uncertain.*)

ADAM: (*Gently*) Come on, Mo, what is it? What's the matter?

MAUREEN: (*In a small voice*) Nothing. I've said it's nothing.

ADAM: Don't keep saying nothing. Something is. Something must be. Come on, what is it? Mo?

(MAUREEN *shakes her head but refuses to answer.*)

Well, I don't know. I don't know what I'm supposed to have said. What am I supposed to have said? Whatever it is I'm supposed to have said, I'm sorry I said it – if I said it.

MAUREEN: You haven't said anything. It's not you. It's not your fault. It's everything.

ADAM: What do you mean, everything?

MAUREEN: It's –

(AGGI, *another waiter, interrupts them.* AGGI *is middle-aged and has adopted the couple ever since they first started eating there together. Indeed, they first fell in love at one of his tables, so he feels responsible for their continuing happiness. He is given to sudden bursts of unaccompanied, full-blooded singing – folk songs in his native tongue – which he fondly hopes will further the course of true love.*)

AGGI: More coffees? Liqueurs? Brandies? Ports? No?

MAUREEN: No.

ADAM: No, thank you.

AGGI: (*Singing softly and with great feeling*) So niss pro nentoy,
Sar beeeeee tarin-tair.
Chin neeee boolentoy,
Oh non tee brunto . . .

(*He finishes, pauses dramatically.*)

30

So.

(AGGI *goes. The pair have barely registered his recital.*)

ADAM: What do you mean, everything?

MAUREEN: It's just your parents and . . .

ADAM: My parents? What about my parents?

MAUREEN: It's all become so – important, hasn't it?

ADAM: How do you mean? You mean to you? Important to you?

MAUREEN: No. To you.

ADAM: Me? I don't care. I don't give a stuff.

MAUREEN: You do give a stuff, that's the point. You give a huge stuff. I wish you didn't.

ADAM: I don't. I do what I like. I always have done. I don't take any notice of them. I don't care what they think.

MAUREEN: But you want them to like me, don't you?

ADAM: I don't mind either way . . .

MAUREEN: You need them to approve –

ADAM: I really don't –

MAUREEN: You do, Adam. You do, you know.

ADAM: I don't know why you should think that.

MAUREEN: Because you keep going on about it. 'Maureen, when you meet them, don't say this, will you? Don't say that.'

ADAM: When did I – ?

MAUREEN: 'Don't wear that, will you, they won't approve of that. Be careful not to swear, will you? Don't say condoms, pessaries and penis in front of my mother, will you?

ADAM: (*Looking round, alarmed*) Sssh!

MAUREEN: I've even dyed my bloody hair for her . . .

ADAM: Oh come on . . .

MAUREEN: It's true.

ADAM: You didn't dye it for her . . .

MAUREEN: Who else? Who else did I dye it this bloody boring colour for?

ADAM: You.

MAUREEN: Me. Why should I do that? I hate it like this. I loathe it. I detest it like this. I can't bear to look at myself . . .

ADAM: Well. For me then.

MAUREEN: Do you like it like this?

31

ADAM: Well, I . . . yes . . .

MAUREEN: Better than the way it was before?

ADAM: Er – well . . .

MAUREEN: Exactly. It's for her. I dyed it for your mother. So I'd look dead ordinary. I haven't even met the woman and I've dyed my hair for her.

ADAM: You didn't need to.

MAUREEN: I did need to.

ADAM: Why?

MAUREEN: Because.

ADAM: Yes?

MAUREEN: Because. I want to be right for you. I want to look right for you. Because it matters so much to you – no don't argue, it does – and it has to be right. You need their approval so I have to be right for you.

ADAM: You are right for me.

MAUREEN: I hope so. I really, really hope I am. I've got all my hopes on you, Adam.

ADAM: So what if they don't approve? What the hell? What's it matter? We'll have to spend next Christmas on our own, won't we? Won't make a scrap of difference to me, the way I feel about you. Just be you, that's all. Be yourself. That's who I fell in love with. That's who I love. Don't you see?

MAUREEN: I hope you believe that.

ADAM: I do. (*Slight pause.*) Well.

MAUREEN: And you think that blue dress I bought will be alright? For this party?

ADAM: It's not a party, I've said. It's just dinner, that's all. Supper. Us six for supper. Here in this restaurant. Quite informal. Nothing flash . . .

MAUREEN: You think that dress is too much, then?

ADAM: It's perfect. Come as you like, they're not fussy. My father never dresses up these days if he can help it. He'll probably come in an old sweater, knowing him . . .

MAUREEN: What about your mother?

ADAM: Well, my mother – yes, she'll probably wear something a bit . . .

MAUREEN: And what about whatsername, your brother's wife?

32

ADAM: Steph? Well . . . she's usually fairly casual. She'll probably wear a dress of some sort . . .

MAUREEN: Short or long?

ADAM: I don't know. Short.

MAUREEN: How short?

ADAM: Well, you know, long short, I don't know. Come in your jeans, what does it matter?

(*Slight pause.*)

MAUREEN: I hope it's not too boring . . .

ADAM: What, the party?

MAUREEN: No, that dress I bought. I don't usually wear things like that. I could maybe put a bit of bright jewellery with it, just to cheer it up.

ADAM: (*Slightly anxious*) Not too much.

MAUREEN: No. Do you think those earrings I wore the other night would do? You know. The parakeets?

ADAM: Oh, yes. The big ones, you mean?

MAUREEN: Yes. Do you think they'd go with it?

ADAM: (*Uncertainly*) Yes.

MAUREEN: No?

ADAM: Have you got any others?

MAUREEN: I'll wear the studs.

ADAM: Wear the parakeets if you like.

MAUREEN: No, they're wrong. They're definitely wrong. I'll wear my opal studs.

ADAM: They're nice.

MAUREEN: You gave them to me. (*Remembering*) Oh, yes, look. Before I forget. (*She rummages under the table for her bag.*) You must tell me – don't be afraid to tell me if this is wrong. If it's wrong I won't be offended. But you must tell me if it's the sort of thing she likes.

(MAUREEN *produces the string plant holder that she will later give to* LAURA.)

(*Holding up the gift*) What do you think?

ADAM: Yes. Yes. (*He studies it.*) What is it exactly?

MAUREEN: It's macramé. It's for holding a plant holder. You put it in here. Then you hang it up. Like that. Do you see?

ADAM: Oh yes, that's great.

MAUREEN: Is it the sort of thing she likes, do you think?

ADAM: Oh, yes. She'll love it.

MAUREEN: Really?

ADAM: Oh, yes.

MAUREEN: I made it myself.

ADAM: Yes.

MAUREEN: I couldn't think what to buy her that wasn't either terribly expensive – and then I thought –

ADAM: You don't have to give her anything, you know. You haven't even met her.

MAUREEN: Oh, I have to give her something if I'm going to her party.

ADAM: It's just supper. There's the book. The poetry book I got her. That could be from both of us, if you want.

MAUREEN: No, I'd like to give her something personal. From me. I think that's important. So long as you think this is right?

ADAM: It's great.

MAUREEN: Took me hours.

ADAM: Yes.

MAUREEN: I kept going wrong. I haven't made one since I was at school. Used to make masses of them at school. All we ever did at school, actually.

ADAM: (*Taking her hands*) It'll be a great evening, you wait and see? Trust me. They'll love you. And you'll love them.

MAUREEN: Yes. You're right. It's going to be *great*, isn't it? And if they don't like me – well fuck 'em.
(*They smile at each other.*)

ADAM: You – er . . . you won't use language like that in front of them, will you?
(*As a frown of uncertainty returns to* MAUREEN'*s face, the lights fade on them. Lights return to the main table where* LAURA *is seated as before. It's a few minutes later.* GERRY *returns immediately. He carries two glasses of brandy.*)

GERRY: Here you are.

LAURA: I said, I didn't want one.

GERRY: You've got it.

LAURA: Remember, you're driving.

34

GERRY: So I am. (*He sits.*) Just been talking to old Ernesto.

LAURA: Oh, yes.

GERRY: He's had a big party on upstairs. They've nearly finished. Said he'd pop down and have a word.

LAURA: We're not going to be too late, are we?

GERRY: Come on. Don't be so bloody miserable. It's your birthday.

LAURA: Only for another twenty minutes, it is.
(*Pause.*)
What was she wearing? What did she think she was wearing?

GERRY: Who?

LAURA: That girl of Adam's.

GERRY: A dress, wasn't it?

LAURA: She must have thought she was going to an embassy cocktail party . . .

GERRY: Showed off a lot of her – Very nice.

LAURA: Thoroughly common. Common as dirt.

GERRY: Oh, I don't think so. Apparently her father breeds race horses.

LAURA: Does he?

GERRY: So she informed me.

LAURA: (*Digesting this*) Well . . .

GERRY: And her mother's a French horn player with the Hallé Orchestra.

LAURA: I find that hard to swallow, I must say.

GERRY: Why should she lie about it?

LAURA: What? All of them living in that little back-to-back on the side of the canal in Harwick Road?

GERRY: (*Shrugging*) Well . . .

LAURA: God, I feel depressed. Why do I feel so depressed?

GERRY: Because you're fifty-four today, my love.

LAURA: That'll do it, dear. Thanks a bunch.

(*Another gloomy silence descends on both of them as the lights cross fade to* STEPHANIE, *who is finishing a grapefruit cocktail in solitary state. She has evidently spent a great deal of time and trouble with her appearance. It is now almost a month later for her, a lunchtime on Friday, 14 February.*
TUTO, *full of the joys of spring as ever, bounces over to her.*)

35

TUTO: Madama, you enjoy that?

STEPHANIE: Yes, it was lovely. Thank you.

TUTO: Can't eat it all, no?

STEPHANIE: A bit too much, that's all.

TUTO: You want to go on? You want to wait for him?

STEPHANIE: Er – I don't know, really. I can't think where he's
    got to.

TUTO: Come on, you go on. You don't wait for him. It's
    Valentine's Day. What sort of husband stand up his
    beautiful wife on Valentine's Day? He don't deserve you, eh?
    (STEPHANIE *smiles faintly*.)
    Tell you what, in half an hour I come off duty, I come and
    eat with you, be your valentine, how about that?

STEPHANIE: I might take you up on that, be careful . . .

TUTO: You want to order?

STEPHANIE: No – I'll just have some water, please. Some still
    water.

TUTO: Still water. Running deep. OK. Right away. (*Seeing
    someone*) Hey look! About time too! What time does he call
    this, eh?
    (GLYN *enters, hurriedly*. TUTO *hovers*.)

GLYN: Sorry, darling.

STEPHANIE: Where have you been? I had to start –

GLYN: (*Kissing her, briefly*) I'm sorry. I promised you lunch and
    then . . .

STEPHANIE: What kept you?

GLYN: Trouble.

TUTO: A drink for seerar?

STEPHANIE: What trouble?

GLYN: Tell you later. Large Scotch with water and I'll order
    straight away.

TUTO: Large Scotch with water, right away. Seerar, the menu.
    Thank you.
    (TUTO *goes off*.)

STEPHANIE: What's the problem?

GLYN: I've been with the auditors . . .

STEPHANIE: And?

GLYN: God knows what the old boy was playing at. Money

missing from here. Money deposited there with no record at all of how it got there. Where it came from. I don't know how he got away with it. Anyway, God knows what we owe, what we're owed – what's in profit . . . what isn't. God knows.

STEPHANIE: But surely he had to keep records? He couldn't just have . . .

GLYN: Oh, there are plenty of records. And at first glance everything's fine. Couldn't be rosier. He'd just taken a number of what he obviously considered were – like, temporary financial emergency measures. He was dead crafty. He was a genius. He's like a man who puts a building up without bothering with walls. It all looks wonderful till somebody tries to stand on the roof.

STEPHANIE: I can't believe he was crooked. Not Gerry.

GLYN: He wasn't crooked. Not at all. Well, no more than most. Better than a lot, really. Only usually they get the chance to tidy things up before they quit. They don't get hurled off the inner ring road in their prime.

(TUTO *returns with a large Scotch and water and a bottle of carbonated water for* STEPHANIE.)

TUTO: One water with Scotch. One fizzy water without Scotch.

STEPHANIE: (*Feebly*) I did ask for – er . . .

TUTO: Seerar, you want to order?

GLYN: Yeah – do you want a starter?

STEPHANIE: No. I've had mine. But you go ahead. You have yours . . .

GLYN: No, we'll go straight to the main course, no problem . . .

STEPHANIE: No, have a starter.

GLYN: Then you'll have to sit and watch me . . .

STEPHANIE: I don't mind.

GLYN: No, we'll both have a main course –

STEPHANIE: No, I don't want a main course . . .

GLYN: You don't want a main course?

STEPHANIE: No.

GLYN: Why not?

STEPHANIE: I just don't.

GLYN: You don't mind if I have a main course?

37

STEPHANIE: No, you have what you like. I say, I'll just have the water.

GLYN: You don't want pudding, either?

STEPHANIE: I don't want anything.

GLYN: Then why the hell do you come out to lunch if you don't want to eat?

STEPHANIE: Why the hell do you think?

GLYN: I can't imagine.

STEPHANIE: (*Angrily*) To see you. How else do I get to see you? Book an appointment?

GLYN: (*Calming down*) OK. Here I am.

TUTO: Seerar. You want to order?

GLYN: Yes, I'll order.

TUTO: You want the special Valentine's Day Meal? Very nice.

GLYN: No, no. Do you have any crimpledoos?

TUTO: Crimpledoos? Oh yes. Freshly made. Very delicious.

GLYN: I'll have a plate of that.

TUTO: Crimpledoos. Nothing for the lady?

GLYN: Nothing for the lady, apparently.

(TUTO *departs*.)

You'll slip through the floorboards at this rate if you don't eat.

STEPHANIE: (*Wryly*) Hardly.

GLYN: You should eat.

STEPHANIE: I do eat.

GLYN: When? When do you eat?

STEPHANIE: I eat when I feel like it.

GLYN: I don't want you getting ill.

STEPHANIE: I'm alright.

GLYN: I've got enough on my plate without an anorexic wife.

(*Slight pause*.)

Sorry. I seem to remember this was supposed to be a romantic little luncheon.

STEPHANIE: Yes.

GLYN: Yes. Sorry. (*He smiles at her*.)

(*She smiles back*.)

How was your morning? Better than mine, I hope?

STEPHANIE: Some of it. I spent the first two hours on the phone to your mother.

GLYN: How is she?

STEPHANIE: Oh, she's perfectly alright. She's decided this week to sell the house and go and live in France, that's the latest.

GLYN: France? I thought it was Italy?

STEPHANIE: No, that was last week.

GLYN: My mistake. Can't keep up with her.

(*Slight pause.*)

STEPHANIE: Actually I'm . . .

GLYN: Hmm?

STEPHANIE: I've – er . . . I don't quite know how you're going to take this. I went to the doctor's this morning and –

GLYN: What for –

STEPHANIE: Well, it was just –

GLYN: (*Angrily*) You are ill, aren't you? I knew this would happen. I said it would happen. I've told you to look after yourself . . .

STEPHANIE: It's alright . . .

GLYN: . . . haven't I told you again and again to eat properly . . . ?

STEPHANIE: . . . it's alright . . .

GLYN: . . . all this bloody stupid slimming –

STEPHANIE: (*Shouting him down*) It's alright. I'm pregnant, that's all, I'm only pregnant, that's all!

(*Silence.*)

GLYN: (*Stunned*) Pregnant?

STEPHANIE: Are you pleased? I hope you're pleased. I am. Well, I am if you are, let's put it that way.

GLYN: I'm –

STEPHANIE: You're angry, aren't you?

GLYN: No, of course not, I'm –

STEPHANIE: You're pleased? You're delighted? You're ecstatic? You couldn't give a toss either way?

GLYN: No, I'm pleased, I'm pleased for you. Of course I am. (*Searching for something to say*) Congratulations.

STEPHANIE: You had a hand in it, too. Well, maybe not a hand but –

GLYN: When did we – when was it we . . . ?

STEPHANIE: I think it was the night of the party – Mother's birthday . . .

39

GLYN: Oh, yes.

STEPHANIE: It had to be. We were in a bit of a hurry . . .

GLYN: (*Smiling*) Yes. Bit drunk.

STEPHANIE: Not that drunk, do you mind?

GLYN: No, not that drunk.

> (*They smile at each other.*)

STEPHANIE: Congratulations to you.

GLYN: Thank you. (*Still taking in the news*) God!

STEPHANIE: That's shut you up, hasn't it?

> (*At this moment* TUTO *arrives with a plateful of something that could be pasta.*)

TUTO: Crimpledoos.

GLYN: Thank you.

TUTO: Benzay appertass!

> (TUTO *goes off.* GLYN *picks up a fork and proffers it to* STEPHANIE.)

GLYN: Listen, half of this is yours. OK?

STEPHANIE: (*Cheerfully*) Benzay appertass!

> (*As they both sit and eat together, the lights fade on them and, simultaneously come up on* ADAM *and* MAUREEN. *Her appearance has undergone a slight change. Indeed, as we progress further back, the real, original* MAUREEN *will slowly be revealed. A much less conventional girl, exotically clad in vivid colours and bold ornamentation. But much of this awaits us in the past. At this point, only her hair colour has changed, back to its original bright shade.*
> *They both wear paper hats, courtesy of the management, and are studying the sweet menus,* MAUREEN *rather listlessly.*)

ADAM: Well? What are you going to have then?

MAUREEN: Nothing.

ADAM: Nothing?

MAUREEN: I'm not hungry.

ADAM: Since when?

MAUREEN: Since now.

ADAM: Five minutes ago you were starving. Couldn't wait to get at the sweet trolley . . .

MAUREEN: Well, I'm not any more.

ADAM: I'm having something.

MAUREEN: Have it.

ADAM: What's got into you all of a sudden?

MAUREEN: Nothing.

ADAM: This is meant to be our Christmas dinner, you know.

MAUREEN: I know.

ADAM: Come on. Happy Christmas, then.

MAUREEN: It's not Christmas, though, is it?

ADAM: Nearly.

MAUREEN: It's December the 20th. That's not Christmas. I want
to spend Christmas with you. Not just December the 20th.

ADAM: Well, you can't. I've said. Not this year. I have to spend it
with my family. I can't just –

MAUREEN: Alright. Spend it with them. But why can't I come as
well?

ADAM: Because. Ours is always a family Christmas. We don't
invite outsiders. It's tradition. It's just family.

MAUREEN: I bet that sister-in-law of yours – what's her name –
your brother's wife –

ADAM: Stephanie.

MAUREEN: Stephanie. I bet that Stephanie will be there?

ADAM: Of course she will. She's family.

MAUREEN: Not really. She's not a blood relation.

ADAM: She's married to Glyn. She's related by marriage . . .

MAUREEN: Well, we're engaged. We're related by engagement.

ADAM: It's not the same thing.

MAUREEN: I bet when she was engaged to your brother, she came
home with him for Christmas.

ADAM: (Warily) I can't remember.

MAUREEN: She did, didn't she? I'm right.

ADAM: It was a long time ago.

MAUREEN: Then why can't I?

(Pause.)

Don't answer.

ADAM: What about your family? Aren't you going home to them?

MAUREEN: I will if you'll come with me.

ADAM: I can't.

MAUREEN: No, of course you can't. Anyway, I wouldn't subject
you to that. I hate them. I hate them all. I hate my sister,

41

she's foul – she's got horrible crinkly hair and pink
wallpaper. And she has this revolting bald husband who puts
glass doors in everywhere and a squealing baby with an
orange face that you really want to sit on. And my mother,
she's vile, she's so low, she's really low. She sits there
smoking these horrible home-made fags and coughing and
complaining. And me grandad's incontinent and the dog's
always got worms and the whole place stinks of stale bacon
fat and I wouldn't go back there if you paid me.
(*Pause.*)
ADAM: I can't keep up with your family.
(*Pause.*)
Every time you tell me about them, they're different.
(*Pause.*)
So you won't be going home, then?
MAUREEN: Probably. I always do in the end. Get pissed with me
grandad. It's alright, really. It soon passes, Christmas,
doesn't it? He's quite funny after three bottles. Anyway, I'll
have to. I can't come home with you because you're ashamed
of me and I'm not staying here on my own, no way.
ADAM: I'm not ashamed of you . . .
MAUREEN: No?
ADAM: I love you.
MAUREEN: I know you do. You're still ashamed of me,
though . . .
(AGGI *enters with the sweet trolley. He is singing a lyrical ballad,
softly and with feeling, especially for them.*)
AGGI: (*Singing*) Selentay . . .
        Corentay . . .
        Passalay . . .
        Unchentay . . .
MAUREEN: Hallo, he's back . . .
AGGI: (*Singing, as he presents them with the sweet trolley*)
        Arrantay . . .
        Novilo . . .
        Decanto . . .
        Devino . . .
    (*Speaking*) Puddings. For the lovers . . .

MAUREEN: No, thank you.

AGGI: No? No love puddings for madametta . . . ?

MAUREEN: No, no love puddings, no thank you, Aggi. Not
    tonight.

AGGI: (*Resuming his song*) Hontay . . .
        Consentay . . .

ADAM: I'll have – what's that one at the top? The chocolate one?
    I'll have a piece of that.

AGGI: Chooker. Delicious.
        (*Singing as he serves it, a new tune*) Telly mat la marracho
            Tenna rastu e lay to . . .
        (*Speaking*) Some cream . . . ?

ADAM: Yes, loads of cream.

MAUREEN: Uggghh!

ADAM: You want a bit?

MAUREEN: No, I don't. (*To* AGGI) Do you have any Christmas
    pudding?

AGGI: Christmas pudding? No, we don't have Christmas
    pudding. Some shups? That is raspberry sponge cake with
    almonds?

MAUREEN: No, I only want Christmas pudding. I won't have
    anything, in that case.

ADAM: Have some wine, there's some wine left here.

MAUREEN: I don't want it. I don't drink, you know that.

ADAM: You do.

MAUREEN: Half a glass. It's not worth it. It has no effect on me at
    all.

AGGI: (*Presenting the sweet with a flourish*) Seerar!

ADAM: Thank you.

AGGI: Some coffee to follow?

ADAM: Maybe in a minute.

AGGI: Then maybe in a minute, I will return. Enjoy! Benzay
    appertass!
        (*Singing*) Hoo tie rooooo,
            Shill leees oh maaayyyy . . .
        (AGGI *goes off with the sweet trolley, singing.*)

MAUREEN: Do you suppose he sings at everybody like that?

ADAM: I don't know.

MAUREEN: Does he sing at your parents, when they come here?

ADAM: I doubt it. I think it's just for us. It's quite romantic.

MAUREEN: Yes, it is. Could get on your nerves after a bit though, couldn't it?

ADAM: I'll ask him to stop –

MAUREEN: No, he's enjoying himself.

ADAM: I thought you liked it.

MAUREEN: I do normally, it's just tonight . . .

ADAM: (*Anxiously*) Are you sorry we got engaged?

MAUREEN: Of course not. I'm very excited we got engaged. It's the most wonderful thing that ever happened to me. It's the only wonderful thing that ever happened to me, as a matter of fact, getting engaged to you . . . I just wish we could –

ADAM: What?

MAUREEN: I wish we could tell somebody else about it.

ADAM: We will.

MAUREEN: When?

ADAM: Soon, As soon as –

MAUREEN: As soon as you've told your parents?

ADAM: Yes.

MAUREEN: And as soon as I've had their seal of approval, presumably. And when will that be – ?

ADAM: Well –

MAUREEN: Oh, God. Don't bother. Give me a spoonful of that and shut up.

(*He offers her a spoonful.*)

I try, you know. Look, I've got my little finger stuck out and everything.

(*She studies him as she eats from his spoon.*)

It's dead important to you, isn't it? That they approve of me? That they like me? Answer me. It is, isn't it?

ADAM: Yes, I suppose it is.

(*A silence.* ADAM *looks very unhappy.* MAUREEN *absently spoons some more pudding off his plate.*)

I love you. I love you so much, you've no idea.

MAUREEN: My God, sometimes parents have a lot to answer for, don't they?

(*She swallows the spoonful of pudding.*)

Hey! This is *good!*

(*She grabs Adam's bowl and sets about the rest of the contents. He watches her, still not very happily. The lights fade on them and come up on* GERRY *and* LAURA. *A silence of several minutes has existed between them ever since we were last with them.*)

GERRY: Well . . . Depressed or not . . . the evening's not been completely wasted. At least we've got them back together . . .

LAURA: (*In her own thoughts*) Mmm?

GERRY: Glyn and Stephanie. And Timmy. At least they're settled.

LAURA: Till the next time.

GERRY: There'll be no next time.

LAURA: You sound very certain.

GERRY: He gave me his word.

LAURA: He what?

GERRY: Glyn. That he wouldn't do it again. He gave me his word.

LAURA: Rubbish!

GERRY: This evening. In the Gents.

LAURA: How can he do that? How can anybody give his word on that? Certainly not Glyn. It's in his nature. First good-looking typist he meets in the lift, he'll have his trousers round his ankles soon as look at her . . .

GERRY: He's not like that . . .

LAURA: Mind you. Married to a dried-up prune of a girl like her, who'd blame him.

GERRY: Oh, come on . . .

LAURA: I'm certain she keeps him on short rations, I'm sure she does . . .

GERRY: How can you know that?

LAURA: You can tell. You can always tell. You can tell from a woman's appetites. She toys with her food, she sips at her wine, she picks at her men.

(*As if to make her point,* LAURA *drains the rest of her brandy glass in a single gulp.*)

GERRY: I've never heard any of this. It's all nonsense.

LAURA: How do you know? You don't know a bloody thing about

women. You never have done. You think we're from another planet. You're not interested in them. Take them or leave them, you. Mostly leave them.

GERRY: How much have you had to drink?

LAURA: Enough. (*Angrily*) It's my birthday, isn't it? What the hell's it to you?

GERRY: Alright. Come on, come on. Simmer down. What's the matter with you?

(*Pause.*)

(*An attempt to lighten things*) Behave yourself, woman. I'll put you over my knee in a minute.

LAURA: Yes, you've done that in your time, haven't you?

GERRY: I have not, what are you talking about?

LAURA: Oh yes, you've hit me before now . . .

GERRY: Rubbish.

LAURA: It's true.

GERRY: Only – only when you drove me to it . . .

LAURA: Only when you cared enough to bother, you mean.

GERRY: (*Muttering*) I don't know why we're dragging this up. It was years ago.

(*Pause.*)

LAURA: No, in that respect – and only in that respect I hasten to add – Glyn's like me. He's inherited my needs. My appetites. We're not the sort to sit and pick at our food. Never have been.

GERRY: What are you talking about? You're both the same as everybody else. We're all made exactly the same. We all want the same thing equally badly. Only some of us control it. Some of us don't. It's strength of mind, that's all it is. I can control it, I've never strayed. I won't say I've never been tempted but I've controlled it. Whereas Glyn obviously can't. Adam, well, I think he probably can, who the hell knows with him? You can, Stephanie can – so far as I know . . .

LAURA: How do you know?

GERRY: What?

LAURA: You're saying this with great authority but how do you know . . . ?

46

GERRY: I think we can safely assume –

LAURA: Well, I don't think you can. And frankly I don't think you should.

GERRY: What is this? Do you know something about Stephanie that I don't know? Has she been carrying on as well?

LAURA: Her? She'd never have the energy to climb the stairs.

GERRY: Then who are we talking about?

LAURA: Never mind. It doesn't matter.

GERRY: No, hold on. Who are we talking about here? Not Stephanie, we've established that. We already know about Glyn. Not Adam, we think. Not me. Who does that leave us with, I wonder?

LAURA: I don't know.

GERRY: (*Staring at her hard*) Who is it?

(LAURA *appears not to hear him.*)

(*Rising*) Who is he, Laura?

(*She continues to ignore him.*)

(*Moving closer to her and bellowing*) Laura, who the bloody hell is he?

(*For a second, he makes as if to hit her but as he does so she turns to face him fully. The expression on her face causes him to check the blow.*)

LAURA: (*Hissing at him with loathing*) Don't you dare. Don't you dare lay one finger on me . . .

(*At this moment,* ERNESTO CALVINU *chooses to join them. He carries a tray with three small glasses and a bottle of his country's finest liqueur.*)

CALVINU: (*As he enters*) My friends . . . My good friends . . . Just in time for the end of the special birthday . . .

GERRY: Ah!

LAURA: Aha!

CALVINU: I bring you a little something to toast. Some Schroopellick Crouscac. Literally, Buds of the Little Blossoms. Delicious . . . (*He puts down the tray.*)

LAURA: How lovely.

GERRY: Wonderful.

CALVINU: (*Kissing* LAURA) For the birthday girl . . .

LAURA: Yes . . .

CALVINU: (*Slapping* GERRY *on the shoulder*) And her lucky, lucky birthday husband. (*He embraces* GERRY *warmly, then starts to pour out three glasses and distribute them*.) A good meal? Yes?

GERRY: Oh, yes. As always, Ernesto . . .

CALVINU: A successful party?

LAURA: Wonderful. (*Accepting a glass*) Thank you.

CALVINU: Now this is special. Very special, special. From my own cellar. It is made only in my village.

GERRY: Really?

LAURA: Well . . .

CALVINU: And it is the tradition, once the cork has left the bottle, it must never return. The bottle must be emptied.

GERRY: Well, we'll do our best . . .

CALVINU: Also. It must be drunk quickly. You must not sip. If you sip Schroopellick it is said a man loses his power and the woman loses her power over the man. Friends, your good health.

(*He drains his glass and looks at them expectantly.* GERRY *sniffs his glass a little cautiously but* LAURA, *without a moment's hesitation, drains her glass in one gulp and slams it down on the table.*)

LAURA: Delicious.

GERRY: (*Following suit*) Very nice.

(*He sits back at the other end of the table from* LAURA. *He likewise puts his glass down on the table. Their eyes meet like two gunfighters.*)

CALVINU: (*Seating himself between them, unaware*) Dear friends, we have all the night, as we say, silently to listen to the wisdom of the wine . . .

(*As he starts to refill their glasses the lights dim on them slightly, but not entirely.*

Simultaneously they come up again on ADAM *and* MAUREEN. *She has successfully polished off his pudding.*)

MAUREEN: That was delicious . . .

ADAM: Listen, I was thinking . . . Just after Christmas, it's my mother's birthday and –

MAUREEN: What date?

ADAM: Er, the eighteenth of January . . .

MAUREEN: Capricorn. She's a Capricorn. Just. On the cusp . . .

ADAM: Oh, yes probably . . . Anyway, we usually have a sort of little party – well, not really a party – an informal supper – here, in this restaurant – and I just wondered – I thought that might be a good occasion for you to meet them. I mean, it wouldn't be any big deal, it would just be casual. It wouldn't, you know, be me bringing you home to meet them or anything . . . I mean, you know . . .

MAUREEN: (*Smiling at him tenderly*) I know. I know what it'd be. Yes, I'd love to come. If you're sure that's alright?

ADAM: Oh yes, that would be tremendous.

(*The lights come up on* GLYN *and* STEPHANIE. *The others also remain lit.*)

GLYN: (*Toasting her with his Scotch*) Here's to him, then . . .

STEPHANIE: Or to her. It may be a her, this time.

GLYN: That'd be nice. Her, then. Here's to her.

STEPHANIE: (*Raising her water glass*) Us.

GLYN: Us.

CALVINU: To love, to friendship, to long life . . .

LAURA: Hear! Hear!

MAUREEN: I wonder what I should wear . . .

(*The lights fade on all three couples to a blackout.*)

ACT TWO

The same. At the main table, it is a few minutes later. The bottle of Schroopellick is half empty. LAURA *and* GERRY *sit as before, two combatants biding their time in an unfinished, interrupted contest.* CALVINU *is blissfully unaware of them. The lateness of the hour and the drink have caused him to fall asleep. He is snoring gently.*

A silence.

The ensuing conversation takes place in furious whispers.

GERRY: Who is it, then?
    (LAURA *does not acknowledge him.* CALVINU *snores.*)
    (*A shade louder*) Who is he?
LAURA: Sssshh!
GERRY: (*Softly again*) Who is he?
    (*No reply.* CALVINU *snores.*)
    Laura!
LAURA: There's no point in talking about it here, is there?
GERRY: Now! I want to talk about it now . . .
LAURA: How can we talk about it now?
    (CALVINU *snores.*)
GERRY: Alright. Come on, we're going home . . .
LAURA: I haven't finished my drink . . .
GERRY: (*Furious*) You heard me – home!
LAURA: Don't you shout at me!
GERRY: I'm not shouting at you. I wish to God I could.
LAURA: Just calm down, calm down, will you. You'll drop dead in a minute.
    (CALVINU *snores.*)
GERRY: Don't worry, I won't be the one who drops dead. Have no fear about that. Whoever he is, he'll be the one that drops dead because I'll murder the bastard. I'll kill him and I'll thrash the living daylights out of you.
LAURA: Oh, shut up. Big talk. Just shut up.
GERRY: I promise. I will.
    (CALVINU *snores.*)

LAURA: You can't murder him, anyway.

GERRY: Why not?

LAURA: Because he's already dead, isn't he? He's been dead since 1974.

(*A silence.* CALVINU *snores.*)

Now simmer down . . . For God's sake.

(*Silence.*)

That's better.

GERRY: I still want to know who he was.

LAURA: What are you planning to do? Go round and beat up his kids?

GERRY: His kids? Do you mean he was married as well?

LAURA: Getting warmer.

(CALVINU *snores.*)

GERRY: Who do we know who lost her husband in 1974?

(*The lights fade on them,* CALVINU *snoring gently,* GERRY *with furrowed brow.* LAURA *surprisingly calm as she helps herself to more liqueur.*

At the same time the lights come up on ADAM *and* MAUREEN *at their table. For them it is three weeks earlier, the evening of Saturday, 30 November. They are both in the middle of their main courses – she with a fish dish, he with a meat course. She is not yet her full exotic self but a toned-down version of how she was on the date they had before this – the previous Saturday, which we shall see shortly. They are clearly deeply, passionately in love. They are eating but their eyes are fixed on each other.*)

MAUREEN: (*Urgently*) I want to make love to you now.

ADAM: Now?

MAUREEN: Yes.

ADAM: Here?

MAUREEN: Yes. I want to take all your clothes off . . . and cover you in gravy . . . and lick, lick, lick . . .

(ADAM *chokes.*)

You alright?

ADAM: (*Weakly*) Yes . . .

MAUREEN: Drink something . . . Something go down the wrong way . . .

ADAM: (*Drinking*) Yes, it's OK . . . Don't do that, not when I'm eating!

(MAUREEN *growls*.)

Now, cut that out. Shall I tell you what I'm going to do to you, then?

MAUREEN: (*Excitedly*) Yes, yes, yes, yes, yes . . .

ADAM: As soon as I've finished my meal . . . I'll tell you . . .

MAUREEN: Get the bill . . . We'll have pudding at home.

ADAM: OK. (*He eats a little faster*.)

MAUREEN: Special pudding. Shaky pudding.

ADAM: Careful. People are watching.

MAUREEN: (*Wiggling in her chair*) Shaky, shaky, shaky pud . . .

ADAM: Oh, this is impossible – I can't finish this . . .

MAUREEN: Good. That was the whole idea.

ADAM: We've paid for all this and we've hardly eaten it . . .

MAUREEN: I've paid for it – my turn. You paid last time. Again –

ADAM: But –

MAUREEN: We agreed. My turn. None of that.

ADAM: Right.

MAUREEN: (*Making to rise*) Come on . . .

ADAM: (*Stopping her*) Mo –

MAUREEN: Yes . . . ?

ADAM: I –

MAUREEN: What is it?

ADAM: I – just wanted to say – I hope we might – make this – sort of more permanent, you know.

MAUREEN: Permanent?

ADAM: Yes.

MAUREEN: Us?

ADAM: Yes. If you'd like that. I would. I'd like to think we could be together regularly.

MAUREEN: Regularly?

ADAM: Yes.

MAUREEN: How regularly? You mean like now? Every Saturday?

ADAM: No. Every day.

MAUREEN: Every night?

ADAM: Yes.

MAUREEN: You mean like living together?

ADAM: Yes – if you like. I thought . . . Here . . . (*He fumbles in his pocket and produces a small box*).) Here –

52

MAUREEN: What's that?

ADAM: Here. (*He gives her the box.*)

MAUREEN: (*Opening the box and staring at the contents*) Oh . . .

ADAM: It's – it's not – it's not necessarily an engagement ring, you
know. It's just a ring. For you. From me.

MAUREEN: Yes. (*Studying it.*) It looks a bit like an engagement
ring to me.

ADAM: Well, it could be. If you like. It's quite a nice one. It's
second hand.

MAUREEN: That doesn't matter, I don't mind that. It's beautiful.
I'll put it on, shall I?

ADAM: If – if you want to . . .

MAUREEN: Listen, if we're doing things properly, aren't you
supposed to ask me something first, before I do . . . ?

ADAM: Oh – yes – er . . .

MAUREEN: Don't worry, you don't have to kneel down . . .

ADAM: Would you – er – would you – like – sort of to – get
engaged – to . . . marry me? Would you?

MAUREEN: Well. I'll need to think about it.

ADAM: (*Suddenly very anxious*) You will?

MAUREEN: (*Carefully*) Yes, you see, I have had several other
offers, Adam . . .

ADAM: (*Crestfallen*) Have you?

MAUREEN: That I never told you about. And to be fair to
everyone concerned, I'll have to put your offer alongside
theirs and then – (*Unable to continue*) Oh God, your face –
yes, of course I will.

ADAM: You will?

MAUREEN: Yes. Please. Please. Please. (*She kisses him.*)

ADAM: Oh, I'm so . . . I'm so . . . Oh, good. Here . . .
(*He helps put the ring on her finger.*)
Come on. Home for pudding. I'll get the bill . . . (*He starts
off swiftly.*)

MAUREEN: Hey, no wait . . . Adam! It's my turn. Don't you dare.
Adam!
(ADAM *has gone.* MAUREEN *rescues her bag from under the
table.*)
Oh, you bastard! (*She glances down at her hand, with*

53

realization.) Hey, he's put it on the wrong finger . . .
(*She smiles, then stops as a thought occurs to her. She stares at the
ring again. She frowns, shrugs and goes off after him a little
pensively. The lights fade on their area and we return to* GERRY,
LAURA *and* CALVINU *at the main table, a few minutes later.*
CALVINU *snores. The others continue to whisper.*)

GERRY: (*Softly, as before*) Who the hell do we know who died in
1974 . . . ?

LAURA: It's all over, it's dead and buried. He's dead and buried.
It's over.

GERRY: It's not over till I say it is.

LAURA: I'm sorry I even mentioned it. Fifteen minutes in the
back of his station wagon, I'm sorry I mentioned it.

GERRY: (*Loudly*) In the back of a station wagon . . . !
(CALVINU *stirs in his sleep.*)

LAURA: Sssshhh!

GERRY: (*Quietly*) I don't believe this.

LAURA: Nor did I at the time.

GERRY: Who the hell do we know who was married, drove a
station wagon and died in 1974 . . . ?

LAURA: I was drunk, that's all, he got me drunk . . .

GERRY: And who drank? Died in 1974 – drank himself to death,
maybe? Married – 1974 – station wagon . . . ?

CALVINU: (*Awakening with a shout*) Pedentaaay! Good health,
friends! Good health! (*Becoming aware of his surroundings*)
Ah! I was sleeping? Yes?

LAURA: Yes.

CALVINU: You should have woken me . . .

LAURA: We didn't like to. You looked so peaceful.

CALVINU: Sometimes, old friends – we are older than sometimes.
Tonight – after a long day – I'm a hundred . . .

GERRY: Yes, I know the feeling . . .

CALVINU: It's been many years, eh?

LAURA: Many years.

CALVINU: Do you know how long I have had this restaurant?

LAURA: A long time.

CALVINU: Thirty-six years . . .

LAURA: As long as that?

CALVINU: (*Sharing out the remainder of the liqueur*) I start it thirty-six years ago with my wife Taisa – you remember Taisa . . .

LAURA: Yes, I do . . . She was beautiful . . .

CALVINU: Ran away with the man from the town hall. Comes to inspect my kitchen, runs away with my wife . . .

LAURA: Yes, I remember . . .

CALVINU: And my cousin was the chef. Rootzer. You remember my cousin Rootzer? Big Rootzer?

LAURA: Oh, yes . . .

CALVINU: God rest his soul . . .

GERRY: (*Suspiciously*) What year did he die . . . ?

CALVINU: Oh, 1978, 9 . . . Long time ago. You, my friends, were practically my first customers . . .

LAURA: We were.

CALVINU: You courted in here . . . You were nearly married here, eh? You bring your children here, your family. Your big boys now. They still come here with their women . . .

LAURA: Yes.

CALVINU: All your family. Your sister from America. She come here.

LAURA: Anthea. Yes, she did.

CALVINU: (*To* GERRY) And your brother – David? It was David, yes . . . ?

LAURA: David, yes.

CALVINU: He was also here . . .

LAURA: Yes.

CALVINU: Ah, so sad. The cruelty of the wine. It can be a friend but it can also be your worst enemy. For a man to die like that – so young, so handsome – in that cruel way – to leave his wife, his children, all his loved ones, his dear brother . . .

GERRY: (*Dead*) David.

CALVINU: (*Startled by his tone*) My friend?

GERRY: David.

CALVINU: I'm sorry, I should not have . . .

GERRY: (*Incredulously*) David? David? (*With a cry*) DAVID? (GERRY *rushes out*.)

CALVINU: I'm sorry, I shouldn't . . . I have upset him, I'm sorry . . . I should not have mentioned David.

55

LAURA: No. It brings back painful memories for him . . .

CALVINU: I know. I'm sorry. It was thoughtless. (*He shakes his head.*) I must cash up. I will see he's alright, don't worry. (*He goes, leaving* LAURA *alone at the table. She sips her drink and waits. The lights fade on her and come up on* STEPHANIE, *who sits alone at her table. For her it is lunchtime on Friday, 24 July that same year. She is six-and-a-half months pregnant and, despite her capacious, loose-flowing maternity clothes, is hot and uncomfortable. She is picking her way through her main course, a salad dish of some description. To accompany it a bottle of water (fizzy). She fans herself with the menu and looks out of the window. In time,* GLYN *hurtles in and sits down opposite her. He is hot and breathless. His jacket is off and his tie loosened.*)

STEPHANIE: Where have you been?

GLYN: I'm sorry.

STEPHANIE: Where have you been?

GLYN: Oh, you have started. Good.

STEPHANIE: I've been here since one o'clock, it's ten to two, where have you been?

GLYN: Where do you think?

STEPHANIE: In the office?

GLYN: Obviously. Where else would I be?

STEPHANIE: I don't know. I wonder, sometimes. I phoned. They said you weren't there . . .

GLYN: When was this?

STEPHANIE: About twenty to one. I phoned to say I might be five minutes late. They said you weren't there. You'd gone out.

GLYN: Oh, yes, I was – I popped down to the site. She should have told you that. The girl's a half-wit.

STEPHANIE: She must be. She said you'd been out since eleven.

GLYN: What does she know?

STEPHANIE: I don't know. More than I do, probably.

GLYN: Oh, come on. Don't start that. No more of that.

STEPHANIE: Alright.

GLYN: That's ridiculous. You're being stupid. Now stop it, do you hear.

STEPHANIE: I'm sorry. (*She rummages in her bag and changes the subject abruptly.*) There was a postcard from your mother.

Arrived just after you left. I thought you'd like to see it.

GLYN: Oh, was there? That's nice. (*Vainly*) Waiter –

STEPHANIE: Here. (*She hands him the card.*)

GLYN: (*Studying the picture*) Oh, look at that. Doesn't it look beautiful? Lucky thing. Dive straight into that today, couldn't you?

STEPHANIE: Yes.

(GLYN *reads the postcard, chuckling now and then.*)

Picked a great time to be pregnant, haven't I? Bang in the middle of a heatwave . . .

GLYN: (*Not looking up*) How you feeling?

STEPHANIE: Like a big wet elephant. Picked a wonderful time . . .

GLYN: Well, to be fair, I don't think it was us who really picked it, did we?

STEPHANIE: No. You're right. We didn't. It picked us. Nothing to do with us . . .

GLYN: (*Not really hearing her as he finishes reading the card*) Oh, that's great, isn't it? She really seems to be enjoying herself, doesn't she?

STEPHANIE: Yes, she does.

GLYN: I know she's my mother and I shouldn't say it, but she's a remarkable woman really, isn't she?

STEPHANIE: How do you mean?

GLYN: Well, look at her. The old man's been buried – what? – barely six months. For over thirty years they were inseparable. Close as that. And somehow or other she's managed to put it all behind her. Pick herself up, get back on her feet, carry on, start a new life. Now, that takes real bottle, if you ask me. That shows true character.

STEPHANIE: You're going to have to do the same, starting next week, aren't you?

GLYN: Right. Dead right. New boss. New job, new title.

STEPHANIE: Is it going to be very different?

GLYN: What, the business, you mean? No, I can't see them making any sweeping changes. Not to Stratton's. I mean, we're basically – in their terms anyway – a smallish but highly efficient business. I mean, we've had a few hiccups in

the last few months but who hasn't lately? Who? I reckon
they're going to leave us very much alone, if you ask me. I
mean, my job won't change. Not essentially. Not a jot.
STEPHANIE: I see. They're not going to get rid of you then?
GLYN: Get rid of me? How do you mean?
STEPHANIE: Well, with being taken over, I thought . . .
GLYN: I'd like to see them try. Whole bloody place would grind
to a halt if they did. I mean, we have men who've worked
there all their lives. First for Dad and latterly for me.
Absolute solid, unswerving loyalty. None of that boss–
employee business. First-name terms, these lads. Try and
get rid of me, they'd have them all out. Anyway, it's not that
sort of take-over. Don't worry. Where's the bloody waiter? –
This place is getting worse, you know . . . We'll have to stop
eating here. It's gone right downhill.
STEPHANIE: Oh, Adam phoned. They can't come to dinner next
Thursday.
GLYN: No? Oh, that's a pity. Why's that?
STEPHANIE: Well . . . Actually, I don't think he and Maureen are
together any more. That's the main reason.
GLYN: (Not that upset) No? Oh, dear. They were getting on so
well. What went wrong? I thought he'd really cracked it, this
time. They were practically engaged, weren't they?
STEPHANIE: They were engaged . . .
GLYN: Well, not officially. Not according to mother, they
weren't.
STEPHANIE: Maureen seemed to think it was official, but I agree
there was a slight difference of opinion . . .
GLYN: Well, what's gone wrong?
STEPHANIE: I don't know. He wants to come round and talk
about it. He's very upset.
GLYN: Oh, poor old Adam. Poor lad. Listen, we ought to take
him out somewhere, somewhere quiet, let him pour it all out
to us, get it off his chest. Probably nothing serious.
STEPHANIE: No, he wants to talk to me on his own. He doesn't
want you there.
GLYN: (Hurt) Oh. OK. Fair enough. The woman's touch, eh?
Let me know if I can help in any way . . .

STEPHANIE: I will.

GLYN: Remind him of the old saying: if your personal life collapses, throw yourself into your work . . .

STEPHANIE: Glyn, he's unemployed . . .

GLYN: He's got plans, though. What about his recording studio idea?

STEPHANIE: What about it?

GLYN: No?

STEPHANIE: What do you think?

GLYN: Well, I don't know. He never sticks at things, that's half his trouble, if you ask me . . . Waiter!

(DINKA *appears*.)

DINKA: What you want?

GLYN: At last! I want to order, what do you think.

DINKA: What you want to order?

GLYN: I don't know. I haven't seen a bloody menu yet, have I?

STEPHANIE: Glyn . . .

DINKA: You want a menu?

GLYN: Yes, of course I want a menu.

DINKA: Then, I get you a menu.

GLYN: Oh, don't bother. What's the special today?

DINKA: Slookick with rice, onion and fresh herb . . .

GLYN: That'll do. Give me some of that.

DINKA: It's all gone.

GLYN: Oh, God in heaven. Get me a menu, then.

DINKA: I get you a menu.

GLYN: This place has gone right off, I tell you. This is the very last time we come here.

(*The lights fade on them as he glares round and* STEPHANIE *continues to toy with her lettuce leaf.*

The lights return to ADAM *and* MAUREEN, *who are back at their table. It is Saturday evening, 23 November, virtually their first proper date together since their initial meeting, a week ago. They are both rather on their best behaviour. He has settled for somewhat conventional clothes, a jacket and tie, presumably to reflect her style of dress of the previous week. This time, though, she has opted for the full, exotic works. A veritable, ultra-modern bird of paradise. She's carrying it off with a certain aplomb,*

*despite feeling a little ill-matched with her partner. They are
eating their first course now – she, chopped fruit of some
description and he, some thick soup.
A slight pause while they eat.*)

ADAM: Is that alright? What you ordered?

MAUREEN: Yes, it's very, very nice, thank you. Extremely
pleasant.

ADAM: Good. This is nice.

MAUREEN: It looks nice.

ADAM: Yes, it is.

(*Pause. They eat.*)

It's a sort of soup.

MAUREEN: Yes.

ADAM: Vegetable. I think.

MAUREEN: Yes. It looks delicious.

(*They eat.*)

This is sort of fruit.

ADAM: Yes.

MAUREEN: I'm not sure what sort, though.

ADAM: I'll ask them. If you like. I'll ask them.

MAUREEN: It could be melon but it tastes a bit like pineapple. I
think there's melon in it, but there's something else as well
with it.

ADAM: Could be pineapple.

MAUREEN: Yes, it could well be pineapple . . .

ADAM: Or perhaps lychees?

MAUREEN: Cheese?

ADAM: No, lychees. It's a Chinese fruit . . .

MAUREEN: Oh, yes. No. I've had lychees. In the Chinese.

ADAM: (*Knowledgeably*) Yes. That's where you tend to get them.

MAUREEN: I don't like them, actually. I always think I'm eating
eyeballs.

ADAM: Really?

MAUREEN: Or something similar . . .

ADAM: What?

MAUREEN: (*Embarrassed*) Nothing . . .

ADAM: Sorry?

MAUREEN: (*Covered in confusion*) Sorry. Nothing. Just my mind.

(*He smiles at her. She attempts to regain her dignity. They eat.*)

ADAM: You look really – very – very attractive. If you don't mind me saying . . .

MAUREEN: Oh, thank you.

ADAM: Terrific. I hardly recognized you.

MAUREEN: Well. I thought I'd make an effort.

ADAM: Yes.

MAUREEN: One of the girls in the salon, she did it for me last night. The hair.

ADAM: Must have taken a bit of time.

MAUREEN: It did. Hours. Specially with my hair.

ADAM: Really?

MAUREEN: Had to sleep last night with my neck on a plank . . .

ADAM: A plank?

MAUREEN: Well, a board. You know.

ADAM: A board?

MAUREEN: A wooden board, you know. To stop it getting flattened.

ADAM: Stop what getting flattened?

MAUREEN: My hair.

ADAM: Oh, I see. (*He ponders.*) Do you have it done like that very often, then?

MAUREEN: No, not very often . . .

ADAM: (*Secretly relieved*) Ah.

MAUREEN: Only when I'm going out somewhere.

ADAM: Ah.

MAUREEN: But I don't go out much.

ADAM: You were out last week.

MAUREEN: Pardon?

ADAM: You were out last week. Here.

MAUREEN: Yes, I know . . .

ADAM: But you weren't dressed like that –

MAUREEN: No, well. That was a blind date, wasn't it? I didn't know who this Robin man was, did I? You don't want to go to a lot of trouble for someone they've fished out of a computer you don't know from – (*She laughs.*) That's quite funny. I was going to say – you don't know from Adam. That's quite funny, isn't it. Adam. You get it?

61

ADAM: I'm – I'm glad you think I'm worth it . . .

MAUREEN: (*Affably*) Well. We'll have to see, won't we? Worth the risk.

(*Pause. They eat.*)

ADAM: Er . . . Where'd you get the plank?

MAUREEN: Pardon?

ADAM: The plank you had to sleep on. Where'd you get it?

MAUREEN: It was my bookshelf.

ADAM: Oh. What did you do with the books?

MAUREEN: Put them on the floor.

ADAM: Ah.

MAUREEN: I've only got three.

ADAM: Oh.

MAUREEN: I prefer magazines, really.

(*A pause. They eat.*)

My dad put it up for me.

ADAM: Sorry?

MAUREEN: The shelf.

ADAM: Your dad? The racing driver?

MAUREEN: No, he's not a racing driver.

ADAM: He's not? I thought . . . ?

MAUREEN: I only said that. I was just trying to impress you. I thought it sounded more interesting.

ADAM: Oh. What does he do then?

MAUREEN: He's a brickie.

ADAM: Oh.

MAUREEN: But he's not working regular. That's why he builds shelves. Whenever he's laid off at home my mother makes him build shelves. We've got thousands of shelves everywhere in our house. She's got a thing about shelves, my mother. Shoves everything on shelves. Shove me on a shelf if she could. (*Pause.*) She's not an ex-ballet dancer either. In case you're wondering. (*Pause.*) But she does work.

ADAM: Where's that?

MAUREEN: Tesco's.

ADAM: Aha. Maybe that's why she's so fond of shelves . . .

MAUREEN: Pardon?

ADAM: Nothing.

MAUREEN: No, she's on the tills.

ADAM: Right.

(*They finish their first courses.*)

MAUREEN: Did you find that person you were looking for last week? The one you needed for your office?

ADAM: No, not yet. I'm seeing one or two more on Monday.

MAUREEN: I hope you're not planning to take them all out to dinner here.

ADAM: Oh no. It was only that particular one. She was very experienced. It would have been quite something to have got her . . .

MAUREEN: Did you manage to catch up with her?

ADAM: No – she's. . . not answering my calls.

MAUREEN: Probably fed up having to pay for her own dinner.

ADAM: Oh no, I'm sure she . . . Anyway, we were offering so little she probably wouldn't have been interested.

MAUREEN: What do you do in your office?

ADAM: We – we've just started a magazine. Sort of arts magazine for this area. Reviews. Articles, interviews. There's a lot going on. Masses. The local press just aren't interested most of the time. Lot of talent around. You'd be surprised. We thought we'd try and encourage it.

MAUREEN: Right. Do people buy it? The magazine?

ADAM: Well. We need more to keep going. But we've started well. We're six per cent above our budgeted circulation figures. Oh, look . . . (*He produces a crumpled, cheaply produced magazine.*) I brought you volume two. In case you wanted to have a look. Here. It's for you.

MAUREEN: (*Gingerly taking it*) Thank you. (*Putting it straight in her bag*) I'll read it. Put it on my shelf. Would you like me to pay for it?

ADAM: Oh, no. Complimentary edition. Please.

MAUREEN: Thank you. Incidentally, I am paying for this evening, though . . .

ADAM: Oh, no please. I insist . . .

MAUREEN: No, you paid last week. Fair's fair.

ADAM: Alright. We'll see.

(*Pause.*)

MAUREEN: (*Looking around*) It's not bad this place. Not too
   stuffy. You come here a lot?

ADAM: Yes, it's my parents' favourite restaurant. We used to
   come here as kids. They used to bring us.

MAUREEN: Us?

ADAM: My brother and I. My older brother, Glyn.

MAUREEN: You like to go where your parents go, do you?

ADAM: Not always, no.

MAUREEN: Is your brother married?

ADAM: Oh, yes.

MAUREEN: Has he got any children?

ADAM: Yes. One.

MAUREEN: How old – ?

ADAM: (*Vaguely*) Oh, about four. Or so. A boy. Timothy.
   Timmy.

MAUREEN: You're an uncle, then?

ADAM: Right.

MAUREEN: What does he do, your brother? Does he run arty
   magazines, as well?

ADAM: Oh no. He's with our firm. With my father's firm.

MAUREEN: What do they do?

ADAM: (*Slightly uncomfortable*) Well, we were originally builders
   but we're also transport and we build leisure centres . . .

MAUREEN: Big, then?

ADAM: Pretty big. I don't have anything to do with it.

MAUREEN: What do they call themselves?

ADAM: – Er . . . Stratton's . . . Stratton Unity . . .

MAUREEN: Stratton's?

ADAM: Yes.

MAUREEN: What, *the* Stratton's?

ADAM: Yes.

MAUREEN: Hang on, that's your name, isn't it?

ADAM: Yes. Adam Stratton, yes.

MAUREEN: And you own that?

ADAM: No, I don't. My family does. My father.

MAUREEN: You must be rolling . . .

ADAM: Oh, no. Well, they are. I'm not.

MAUREEN: They're massive. Stratton's. Huge.

64

ADAM: Pretty big.

MAUREEN: Bloody hell. Why am I offering to pay for your dinner? (*She studies him.*) I didn't realize I was out with a Stratton.

ADAM: Well . . .

MAUREEN: If you don't mind me saying so, you could afford a better jacket, couldn't you?

ADAM: Oh, don't you . . . ?

MAUREEN: It's terrible. Even my dad wouldn't be seen dead in that.

ADAM: I'm sorry . . .

MAUREEN: It's all right. I didn't come out with you for your jacket . . . (*She smiles.*)

(ADAM *smiles.*)

Which is just as well. And I didn't come out because you were rich, either, because I didn't know who you were when I said yes and it wouldn't have made any difference even if I had done and I'm still paying half . . .

ADAM: Fair enough. And I'm not rich. You don't get rich running arts magazines.

MAUREEN: Amaze me with some more little known facts.

(AGGI *returns to clear their plates.*)

AGGI: Madametta . . . Seerar . . . You finish? You enjoy? Yes?

MAUREEN: Very much. Thank you?

ADAM: We wanted to know, what was the fruit? The lady's fruit?

AGGI: The lady's fruit? It is – er . . . melon . . .

MAUREEN: Melon, yes. I got that one.

AGGI: With some – pine-apple . . .

MAUREEN: Pineapple. Yes, I said it was pineapple . . .

AGGI: And the juice of – er . . . passion fruit.

MAUREEN: Passion fruit?

AGGI: It's good, eh? It's good for tonight? Passion fruit?

MAUREEN: I don't know about that. He's a bit cheeky, isn't he?

ADAM: Oh, don't mind him, he's always . . .

AGGI: (*Bursting into a loud, full-blooded love ballad*)

   . . . tennesta limpa . . .

   Consensa far ma plea . . .

   Inento! . . . inento! . . . inento!

MAUREEN: (*During this*) He's mad, as well.

ADAM: No, he's . . .

MAUREEN: I feel stupid . . .

> (*As* AGGI *finishes his recital, on bended knee, he presents* MAUREEN *with a flower from the vase on their table.*)
> Thank you. Thank you very much.

AGGI: Deveena Madametta – pulchrosia . . .

MAUREEN: Lovely, yes. Hell, I'm not coming here again . . .

AGGI: Passion fruit! I fetch your main course.

ADAM: Please.

> (AGGI *goes off with the empty dishes.*)
> Sorry about that.

MAUREEN: It's alright, really. It was funny, really. You say your family have been coming here for years?

ADAM: Oh, yes. Since before I was born.

MAUREEN: You must have a funny family, then.

ADAM: Yes. Fairly funny. Sometimes.

MAUREEN: I'd like to meet them. You know, just to meet them. Not – you know.

ADAM: Yes. Maybe. I mean . . .

MAUREEN: I don't have to look like this . . . I mean, if you think that would frighten them . . .

ADAM: No. Of course not . . .

MAUREEN: I've got a proper dress somewhere. My mother bought it me. A really boring one, I promise. It'd go with your jacket.

ADAM: I'm burning this tomorrow.

MAUREEN: No, don't. I like it really. It reminds me of our dog's blanket.

ADAM: Oh, leave it out . . .

MAUREEN: Sorry.

ADAM: You have a dog?

MAUREEN: No, just a blanket.

ADAM: Ah.

MAUREEN: He got run over. But my mother's sentimental. She still keeps his blanket.

ADAM: On a shelf?

MAUREEN: (*Laughing*) Where else?

66

(*They both laugh. Suddenly she leans forward and kisses him lightly on the lips. She sits back. They look at each other.*)
Oh well. The night is young, as they say.

ADAM: It is.

MAUREEN: Haven't got to the pud yet, have we?
(*They continue to smile at each other as the lights fade on them. Simultaneously we return to the main table where* LAURA *is still seated. Half an hour has passed.*
GERRY *returns slowly. His manner is subdued. He sits at the table.*)

LAURA: (*After a second*) Where have you been?

GERRY: For a walk. I needed some air.

LAURA: You've been gone ages. I thought you'd drowned yourself.

GERRY: I might have done. I could well have done.

LAURA: Oh, don't be so melodramatic.

GERRY: I've reason to be, haven't I? I discover, after thirty-two years, my whole marriage is based on a lie. I've been betrayed by my wife – with my own brother . . . My whole personal life been made a mockery . . .

LAURA: (*Impatiently*) Oh, for God's sake. Fifteen minutes. That's all it was. In 1974. A month before he died, poor bugger. From the little pleasure we had from it, it probably helped him on his way.

GERRY: God, you're a cold woman sometimes, aren't you?

LAURA: It's the truth. Come on, don't be so stupid. It was nothing.

GERRY: Then why bother telling me if it was nothing?

LAURA: I don't know. I thought it might amuse you.

GERRY: (*Outraged*) Amuse me?

LAURA: Well, it was long enough ago. (*Laughing*) It was very funny, actually . . .

GERRY: (*Angrily*) I don't want to hear! You think it's a joke? It's not a joke.

LAURA: No, alright. I'm sorry.

GERRY: It may be a joke for you. I have to face people tomorrow, you know.

LAURA: What are you talking about?

GERRY: People sniggering behind their hands.

LAURA: Don't be so stupid. How can they, they don't even know about it.

GERRY: How do I know that for certain?

LAURA: Well, I've never told anyone except you, and you've only just heard about it and he's dead so who else is there?

GERRY: Did no one see you? You know . . . doing it?

LAURA: Of course they didn't.

GERRY: Where did it happen? Where was this station wagon parked?

LAURA: I thought you didn't want to hear . . .

GERRY: Where?

LAURA: Holly Lane.

GERRY: Holly Lane?

LAURA: Back of the social club. In the members' car park.

GERRY: Oh, my God! Our own social club. (*Calming again*) In that case, how can you be sure no one saw you?

LAURA: They didn't. We'd have heard about it by now if they had.

GERRY: Was it very dark?

LAURA: It wasn't dark at all, it was lunchtime.

GERRY: Lunchtime!

LAURA: Sunday lunchtime.

GERRY: Sunday lunchtime? Where was I during all this, then?

LAURA: In the club bar.

GERRY: I see.

LAURA: Drawing the cricket club raffle . . .

GERRY: I see. And there's a lull in the proceedings so you two both went out there and then and had it, did you?

LAURA: Well, he asked me first.

GERRY: That was decent of him. Always the gentleman, my brother. What did he say?

LAURA: (*Vaguely*) He said, 'Come on, what about it?' I think. Something like that. He was never one for speeches, David, was he?

GERRY: Man of few words?

LAURA: Right.

GERRY: Quite a bit of action, though.

LAURA: (*Dryly*) Not a lot of that either, as I remember. Poor man.
GERRY: (*Wearily*) I don't know what to say.
LAURA: Come on, what's the matter with you? Once in thirty-two years. Come on. Hardly makes me Jezebel, does it?
GERRY: You say once. How do I know that?
LAURA: Because I never lie to you. I never have.
GERRY: You lied to me about him, didn't you? About David?
LAURA: No, I didn't. I just never told you about him at all. That's not the same as lying.
GERRY: Don't play with words. Don't try and get clever with me.
LAURA: There's been no one else. Ever. Alright?
GERRY: Well, I can't believe you. I'm sorry.
LAURA: (*Suddenly furious*) Then you're a bloody fool, aren't you? That's all. If you knew how faithful I've been to you over the years . . . Oh no, not just sexually – but that as well – standing up for you time after time, fighting your corner even when I knew you were in the wrong . . . And you just took it, as if it was yours by right. Your right that I'd always be there whenever I was wanted, saying what I was expected to say, doing what I was expected to do. And never once – Well, bugger you, that's all I can say, bugger you!
(*Silence. They are both a little surprised by her outburst.*)
(*Quietly*) And I'm sorry for swearing.
(LAURA *rises suddenly, taking up her handbag and scrabbling inside for a tissue. It is apparent she is about to cry but doesn't want to do so in front of him.*)
GERRY: Where you going?
LAURA: To the Ladies' room. (*She turns, rather tearful now.*) You wouldn't even let me have a dog, would you? You know how much I love dogs . . .
(LAURA *goes out.*)
GERRY: (*Muttering to himself*) I hate bloody dogs . . .
(*He continues to sit there, thoughtful, as the lights fade and come up on* GLYN *and* STEPHANIE's *table. It is again lunchtime, this time on Friday, 6 November.* STEPHANIE *is, as usual, at the table on her own. This time, though, there is evidence that she has not been eating alone and that* GLYN *has simply slipped away for a second. Stephanie has had her second child but she has failed to*

regain much of her figure. She looks a mess, post-natally
depressed, neglected by others and herself. The pair have all but
finished their meal – poised between main course and sweet.
A moment and then GLYN *returns. He has been on the phone*
and has his filofax in hand.)

GLYN: OK. All settled. She'll be here in ten minutes. She'll
pick me up, take me back to the house. I can be packed and
out of there in half an hour, before you get home. No trace.
OK?

STEPHANIE: (*Dead*) Good.

GLYN: Now, this is what we agreed, alright? This is what we
both want.

STEPHANIE: Right.

GLYN: I'm not doing anything that we haven't agreed on
between us? Right?

STEPHANIE: Right.

GLYN: It's best for you, it's best for the kids, it's best for me –

STEPHANIE: And best for her.

GLYN: I don't think she enters into this, do you . . .

STEPHANIE: Oh, I think she probably does, you know.

GLYN: (*Determinedly ignoring her sarcasm*) It's not like I'm
leaving. I'm not walking out on you. I am not abandoning
you. I gave my word on that and I stand by my word. I am
still there when you need me, at the end of the phone, night
or day, rain or shine. And you come first, Steph. You know
that. You and Timmy and little Jess will always come first.
I have made that crystal clear to Sarah. She is strictly
number two in the pecking order . . .

STEPHANIE: Number four . . .

GLYN: What's that?

STEPHANIE: Number four. You said she was number two. She's
number four in the pecking order.

GLYN: (*Slightly impatiently*) Alright then, number two, number
four, have it your way, who's counting? The fact is, if the
crunch comes, she waits strictly in line. She knows that . . .

STEPHANIE: Poor thing . . .

GLYN: (*Admonishingly*) Now, Steph . . .

STEPHANIE: Sorry.

GLYN: Don't spoil it now. We're handling this well between us. We both are. Don't spoil it.

(TUTO *enters*.)

TUTO: Madama, seerar. You want a sweet? You want to see the sweet trolley?

GLYN: Not just at the moment, thanks.

TUTO: You want just coffee?

GLYN: In a minute.

TUTO: OK.

(TUTO *goes off again*.)

GLYN: Now, is there anything you want me to do before I go?

STEPHANIE: No.

GLYN: You got my number?

STEPHANIE: Yes.

GLYN: And you're not to worry about money, either. I won't keep you short. You'll probably find you're better off, anyway, without me to worry about. Well, it may get a bit tight, I admit, for a week of two – until I've got this problem at work sorted out . . . But there's no way they're going to treat me like that and get away with it. I am demanding full compensation and I intend to fight them till I get it. And I don't mean an offer of a so-called golden handshake where all I finish up with is two fingers. No, we'll survive, never fear. There's a lot of people showing interest in me at the moment. Word's got round I'm on the market. I'm not going to be short of offers, don't worry. Some of these little firms, they'd give anything to get a Stratton on their board . . . Boost their credibility no end.

STEPHANIE: (*Dully*) Your mother's back, did you know? She phoned me last night.

GLYN: Yes. I was going to tell you that. I popped up to see her this morning.

STEPHANIE: With *her*?

GLYN: What?

STEPHANIE: Did you go up to see your mother with *her*?

GLYN: (*As casually as he can*) Yes, as a matter of fact Sarah was with me, yes.

STEPHANIE: Didn't your mother think that was odd? You coming to see her with Sarah?

71

GLYN: Well, she didn't remark on it – but you know my mother, she's very discreet . . .

(STEPHANIE *laughs*.)

She asked after you. How you were.

STEPHANIE: Oh, that's nice.

GLYN: Wanted to know how Timmy was. How much he'd grown since she's been away. And of course she's desperate to see little Jess.

STEPHANIE: I bet.

GLYN: You'll try and get up to see her, won't you?

STEPHANIE: Maybe.

GLYN: Well, you've got the car, Steph, haven't you? I left you with the car, for God's sake. Think about me. No car at all.

STEPHANIE: You'll have to make do with her car then, won't you?

GLYN: (*Laughing*) I don't know about that. I think my days with open top convertibles are strictly numbered. (*Sincerely*) Do try to get up to see mother, Steph. It would mean a lot to her, it really would. She's looking great by the way. Fantastic suntan. Had her hair re-coloured. Looks about twenty years younger. I said to her, you're back in with a chance, Mum.

STEPHANIE: (*Murmuring*) Lucky man.

GLYN: Lucky man, yes. (*Craning round*) Must keep an eye out for Sarah. I don't know if she'll come in here or park outside . . . Oh, Adam was there, too. Saw him briefly.

STEPHANIE: He's back home with her again, is he?

GLYN: Yes. Temporarily. Mum's thrilled to bits, of course. Her chance to spoil him. He's talking of going to night school. To study architecture.

STEPHANIE: Architecture?

GLYN: I said, good for him, the way things are going at the moment I could do with a good cheap house . . . (*Catching sight of someone*) Ah! Here she is. OK. (*Rising*) As I say, I'll be in and out in half an hour. I'll just take my clothes, my personal things. Everything else is yours, OK? As we promised.

STEPHANIE: Right.

GLYN: Don't bother about the bill, I'll . . . (*Suddenly moved*) You've been amazing, Steph. Absolutely amazing over all

this. Thank you. I won't forget it. I mean it. Thank you.
(*He considers kissing her but, realizing this might be altogether
too much, finishes by giving her an affectionate pat on the
shoulder. Then he is gone.*

STEPHANIE *sits frozen, expressionless. In a moment,* TUTO
returns with the sweet trolley.)

TUTO: (*Cheerfully*) Where's seerar? He's gone?

(STEPHANIE *nods.*)

You want to wait for him?

(STEPHANIE *shakes her head.*)

He's coming back?

(STEPHANIE *shakes her head.*)

You want a sweet?

(STEPHANIE *nods.*)

What you like? We have the specialities. Smooliboos. That is
cream with meringue?

(STEPHANIE *nods.*)

OK, you like that? (*Starting to serve*) You want something
with it? Something else? Some delicious trickletasse? This is
delicious tart with treacle and cream mixed with passion
fruit, fresh strawberries and Armagnac . . . ?

(STEPHANIE *nods. She is beginning to cry quietly.*)

(*Oblivious to this*) Yes, OK. Some trickletasse. What else can
we tempt you? Some profiteroles? Some lemon mousse?
Some fruit salad?

(STEPHANIE *continues to nod automatically.*)

You want some of those as well? What, all of them? My God,
lady – when you last eat . . .? (*Ladling things on to the plate*)
OK. Profiteroles . . . and some lemon mousse . . . and a little
fruit salad . . . wow! You want cream? (*Before she can reply*)
Of course you want cream. (*Placing the plate in front of her*)
Madama! Benzay appertass . . . Madama?

(*He notices for the first time that she is crying. Her sobs now
become louder and slowly more convulsive.*)

(*Alarmed*) Madama? (*Gently*) It's OK. It's OK. Don't cry
now. It's OK. I get a doctor, OK? You'll be OK, OK? OK.
(*Calling*) Bengie! Chetti Seerar Calvinu – telephon medicanti
– medicanti – medicanti, yeah.

(TUTO *returns to* STEPHANIE.)

It's alright. Someone's coming. It's OK.

(*He touches her arm to console her.* STEPHANIE *in her desolation, though still seated, turns and clings to him, burying her face in his jacket and continuing to weep.* TUTO, *rather embarrassed, stands patting her ineffectually.*)

It's OK. It's OK. It's OK.

(*The lights fade on them and return to the main area, where* GERRY *is still seated. Five minutes or so have passed.* LAURA *returns.*)

LAURA: Well, have you calmed down, then?

GERRY: (*Indignantly*) Me?

LAURA: I hope you have.

(*Slight pause. She sits again.*)

We ought to go, you know. I think they're wanting to close up.

GERRY: Did you really think it wouldn't matter to me? Telling me about you and David?

LAURA: Well, does it?

GERRY: Of course it does.

LAURA: Oh, come on. It isn't as if we're great lovers, is it?

GERRY: Maybe we aren't now, not now. But in 1974 we were.

LAURA: We weren't.

GERRY: In 1974 we were still . . .

LAURA: We were not.

GERRY: What are you talking about?

LAURA: We bought single beds in August 1970. It's engraved on my memory. I remember saying to myself, goodbye the swinging sixties . . .

GERRY: 1970?

LAURA: August 21, 1970. Friday.

GERRY: Have you written all this down?

LAURA: You remember these things. I do.

GERRY: We bought single beds because of your back.

LAURA: That was the official reason given at the time.

GERRY: We've made love since 1970, for God's sake.

LAURA: Oh, yes. On and off. But we're not great lovers, that's what I'm saying. There's not some burning passion where we

74

can't bear to be out of each other's sight. We don't go mad
with jealousy every time we see one of us talking to someone
else who's half-way attractive.

GERRY: We did. We used to . . .

LAURA: Oh, we did . . . There's one or two of them nearly
finished up in a bin liner, I can tell you . . . Girls after you.

GERRY: Really? I didn't know about this . . .

LAURA: No, you didn't . . .

GERRY: Who were these, then?

LAURA: Never mind.

GERRY: And you saw them off?

LAURA: Oh, yes.

GERRY: How'd you do that?

LAURA: There are ways. A quiet word in the toilet and a bottle of
nail polish remover . . . Works wonders.

GERRY: (*Impressed*) Bloody hell! You did that? For me?

LAURA: We were only kids . . .

GERRY: You loved me that much?

LAURA: I wanted you that much.

GERRY: But you did love me?

LAURA: At that time, I just wanted you. I was far too frightened
of you then to love you . . .

GERRY: Frightened?

LAURA: Oh, yes. You were a frightening young man. Leader of
the pack, you. King of the Teds, weren't you?

GERRY: Teddy Boy King. Right. Remember those shoes? That
thick the soles were.

LAURA: I remember the hair-do.

GERRY: God, what a sight. What did you see in me?

LAURA: (*A fond memory*) You were – dangerous. So dangerous.

GERRY: Never.

LAURA: Oh, you were. I remember those first few times you took
me out. I nearly wet myself I was so frightened.

GERRY: Of me?

LAURA: Yes.

GERRY: Why?

LAURA: I don't know.

GERRY: Then why did you come out with me?

LAURA: Because I loved it. I loved every terrifying minute of it.

GERRY: But you didn't love me?

LAURA: Not then. Later. When I realized you were really a softy.

GERRY: I loved you.

LAURA: Yes, I know you did.

(*A slight pause.*)

Anyway – how did we get on to all that, for God's sake – ? All I was saying was . . . we've both moved on. There's nothing wrong in that, it's called a marriage . . . We're no longer lovers – we're . . .

GERRY: We're what?

LAURA: We're a partnership.

GERRY: You make it sound like a business arrangement.

LAURA: Well, it is in a way – God, you men you're so bloody romantic, aren't you? – of course it's a business. Partly. I hope there's more to it than just that but it's an important side of it, isn't it? It's a legal arrangement. It's a contract. We've entered into it, we traded and in due course we diversified –

GERRY: Diversified?

LAURA: We had the boys . . . and then they occupied our attention . . . Our interest became largely in them, instead. Or, in my case, I have to confess, in Adam. You know how I feel about Glyn.

GERRY: Yes, I do. But I don't pretend to understand it. Your own son.

LAURA: I've never hidden it. Well, I've tried to from him, obviously, but . . . I don't know. There's no logical reason why parents should automatically love their children, is there? Really? I couldn't stand him when he was born. And now he's grown up thoroughly dull and conventional, no creativity, no scrap of imagination – he's always had everything he wanted – thanks to you – and he thinks the world owes him a living. He's treated that marriage of his like a one-night stand –

GERRY: I don't think you can blame him entirely . . .

LAURA: Oh, I don't. He chooses to marry a girl like Stephanie he gets what he deserves. She's as selfish as he is and hasn't got a

76

brain in her head. She can't even cook, they have to eat out half the time. But I told him, he picked her, he sticks with her . . . Those are the rules. He might as well do one thing right in his life. We stuck by them, why shouldn't he?

GERRY: Well. At least we have a grandchild. She's given us that.

LAURA: Yes, well that's nice for you, anyway.

GERRY: And for you?

(LAURA *doesn't answer*.)

Having Timmy? That's nice for you too, isn't it?

LAURA: You know how I feel about babies. I managed with my own – just . . .

GERRY: You like them on television . . .

LAURA: I love them on television. It's having to hold them in the flesh. Oh, don't worry, I'll come into my own with Timmy when he's about fifteen – if I'm still around, that is.

GERRY: You may not love him but Glyn loves you, you know.

LAURA: Really?

GERRY: Much more than he does me. He needs your approval, Laura. He always needs that.

LAURA: That's not quite the same as loving me, is it? Anyway, we can't change the way we are. I can't pretend to love him if I don't, can I? Now, Adam I do love. I understand him. And I think he loves me . . . He's a fool, sometimes, but at least I understand him.

GERRY: I'm glad you do.

LAURA: And I can still be of use to him, I know I can. He's got something, that boy. Real potential. And I'm going to make sure he gets the chance to realize it. Doesn't get trapped by some ambitious little nobody, like that one.

GERRY: Now, be fair. How do you know she's that . . . ?

LAURA: Because I recognize her. From thirty years ago . . . Nothing changes.

GERRY: What're you going to do, then? Have a quiet word with a bottle of acetone?

LAURA: If need be.

(*A silence.* GERRY *stares at her. She sounds as if she means it.*)

(*Without moving*) We must go.

GERRY: Just finish this off.

77

LAURA: You're driving.

GERRY: So what? Nothing on the road, this time of night.

(*He refills his glass. They sit in silence. The lights cross fade to* MAUREEN, *who is sitting at her table on her own. It is now the Saturday, 16 November of the previous year.* MAUREEN *has a pre-dinner drink but has yet to order. She is dressed very conventionally for her. She wears a red flower prominently in her jacket button hole.*

DINKA, *who, unfortunately for her, seems to be her waiter for the evening, enters with a menu.*)

DINKA: (*As gracelessly as ever*) You want to order?

MAUREEN: No, I've said, I'm waiting for someone.

DINKA: Someone else?

MAUREEN: Yes.

DINKA: Someone particular or just someone?

MAUREEN: (*Indignant*) Of course someone particular, what do you think?

DINKA: I don't know.

MAUREEN: I'm not just sitting here on the off-chance, you know. What do you think I am?

DINKA: What time he come?

MAUREEN: He was supposed to come half an hour ago.

DINKA: What he look like?

MAUREEN: He's – he's . . . I'm not sure. I haven't – Well actually, if you must know I have never met him before. But he should be wearing a flower like this one . . .

DINKA: (*His suspicions confirmed*) Uh-huh.

MAUREEN: It's perfectly proper, there's nothing . . .

DINKA: Alright. You behave. You cause trouble, I fetch Mr Calvinu, OK? You go out in the road rightaway.

MAUREEN: Listen, pigface, don't be so sodding rude, alright? Why don't you just go and –

DINKA: (*Holding up a warning finger*) Behave!

(*He goes.*)

MAUREEN: (*Draining her glass, muttering*) Right, that's it. I'm not staying in this place. If he can't be bothered to turn up, that's it.

(*She is about to rise when* ADAM *enters. He carries a folder.*)

ADAM: (*Seeing her*) Ah!

MAUREEN: (*Seeing him*) Oh!

(*For the ensuing dialogue,* MAUREEN *makes a marked effort to 'improve' her speech.*)

ADAM: Hallo.

MAUREEN: Hello.

ADAM: Are you who I think you are? Miss – ?

MAUREEN: (*Overlapping*) Yes, yes. You'll be – ?

ADAM: Yes. Sorry, am I late?

MAUREEN: Well, a little bit –

ADAM: I am sorry. Not a good start. Sorry. (*Extending his hand*) Adam –

MAUREEN: Adam?

ADAM: Yes.

MAUREEN: I thought you were Robin?

ADAM: Robin? No, Adam.

MAUREEN: Adam?

ADAM: Yes.

MAUREEN: Yes. Right. (*Holding out her hand*) I'm Mo'reen . . .

ADAM: Sorry? Marine?

MAUREEN: No, Mo'reen . . .

ADAM: Oh, Mo'reen. Yes, right. Should we sit down?

MAUREEN: Yes, of course.

(*They both sit.* ADAM *opens his folder and looks at the first sheet.*)

ADAM: So that's how you pronounce it, is it? Mo'reen?

MAUREEN: Yes. Usually, yes.

ADAM: (*Reading*) M-Y-F-A-N-W-Y. Mo'reen. Unusual.

MAUREEN: Pardon?

ADAM: That's the correct Welsh way, is it?

MAUREEN: Welsh way? What Welsh way?

ADAM: In Welsh. You are Welsh, I take it? With a name like – Mo'reen – I'd have guessed you were Welsh.

MAUREEN: No.

ADAM: What are you then?

MAUREEN: My father is Irish. Through and through. And my mother is very slightly French.

ADAM: I see. (*He is perplexed.*)

(*Slight pause.*)

MAUREEN: My father's a racing driver.

ADAM: Goodness.

MAUREEN: Formula One.

ADAM: How exciting.

MAUREEN: Worrying, sometimes.

ADAM: Yes. Must be. Especially for your mother.

MAUREEN: Yes.

(Slight pause.)

She's an ex-ballet dancer.

ADAM: Sorry? A what?

MAUREEN: An ex-ballet dancer . . .

ADAM: Oh, ex-ballet dancer, yes. Sorry I thought you said an ex-belly dancer. *(He laughs.)*

MAUREEN: *(Smiling, unamused)* No.

ADAM: Yes. I'm sorry, I had completely the wrong picture of you in my head. From the description I was given of you.

MAUREEN: Description? Oh, you mean the print-out?

ADAM: The what?

MAUREEN: The computer print-out. You got one on me, did you?

ADAM: No.

MAUREEN: I got one on you.

ADAM: Did you?

MAUREEN: Nothing personal. Just the broad details. Mind you, half of them were wrong. I don't think I'd have recognized you, either.

ADAM: No?

MAUREEN: You weren't even wearing your flower, were you?

ADAM: *(Completely lost)* No.

MAUREEN: I suppose if you'd been smoking your pipe I might have recognized you, I suppose.

ADAM: My pipe?

MAUREEN: Yes.

ADAM: I don't smoke a pipe.

MAUREEN: Well, they've certainly got it wrong, haven't they?

(DINKA enters with a menu, again.)

DINKA: You want to order?

ADAM: Well, I think we might like a drink first, mightn't we?

DINKA: *(Recognizing ADAM)* Oh, 'syou.

ADAM: Yes. Good evening.

DINKA: You with *her*?

ADAM: Yes.

DINKA: (*To* MAUREEN) You find someone, then?

ADAM: What? What's he saying?

MAUREEN: (*Coolly*) I've no idea what he's saying.

DINKA: (*To* MAUREEN) You got lucky, eh?

ADAM: I'm sure you'd like another drink? What's that you're having?

MAUREEN: This? Oh, this is just tonic water, thank you.

DINKA: Tonic water. Cheap.

ADAM: Well, I think we should have something a bit more . . . What about – ? What could we have? Kir Royale, perhaps?

MAUREEN: Kir . . . ?

ADAM: Yes, come on, why not?

MAUREEN: Alright.

ADAM: Two Kir Royale.

DINKA: Two Kir Royale. You buying Kir Royale for *her*?

ADAM: Yes.

DINKA: (*Shrugging*) Two Kir Royale . . .

(DINKA *goes off*.)

ADAM: Do you know him? That waiter?

MAUREEN: I certainly don't . . .

ADAM: Funny, he seems to know you. Odd. Anyway. A little bit about me, shall I? While we're waiting. I mean, you've already told me something about you – and anyway – as you're probably aware – you've already got quite a reputation within the business, anyway.

MAUREEN: Pardon?

ADAM: Well, in your own field. You must be conscious of that? I mentioned your name to one or two close colleagues, they were really impressed . . .

MAUREEN: Colleagues?

ADAM: Anyway. Briefly. This is the set-up. Basically, there are the four of us . . .

MAUREEN: Four?

ADAM: All together in the same room. Practically in each other's laps.

MAUREEN: Laps?

ADAM: It's a madhouse. Not the sort of set-up you're used to, I'm sure?

MAUREEN: No, not at all.

ADAM: And we all need looking after in our different ways. Though hopefully not all at once. Well, not that often. We'd all have call on your services, we'd all have access to your expertise . . .

MAUREEN: Just a minute. Let's get this clear. Are we talking about you and three others?

ADAM: Yes. Is that a problem?

MAUREEN: Three other men?

ADAM: Oh, no, no, no. I thought I explained. There's me. And Daniel, who's overall in charge. And then there's Patricia – Trish – and then there's Carmen who deals with the advertising.

MAUREEN: Women as well?

ADAM: Yes.

MAUREEN: You're joking.

ADAM: What is it? Do you not work well with women?

MAUREEN: I bloody don't.

ADAM: (*Dismayed*) Oh. Oh, God. That is a drawback. I had no idea.

MAUREEN: What's supposed to happen, then? You two men stand watching, I suppose . . .

ADAM: What?

MAUREEN: While we three get down to it? That the idea?

ADAM: No. Not at all. God, no, we all muck in together. There's none of that male-female business – not in that place. If something needs doing, whoever's free, they get stuck in and get on with it.

(MAUREEN *gets up*.)

Where are you going . . . ?

MAUREEN: (*Coldly*) Goodnight.

ADAM: Just a minute, don't you –

MAUREEN: Thank you so much. No, thanks. Goodbye.

(MAUREEN *stalks out. She passes* DINKA, *who is carrying a tray with the two glasses of Kir. He stares at her.* ADAM *stands bemused.*)

ADAM: Where is she – ? What have I – ?

DINKA: She gone?

ADAM: Yes. I think so, she – I don't quite know why. She – Why did she walk out like that? Have you any idea?

DINKA: (*Helpfully*) You didn't offer enough money, who knows?

ADAM: No, we never got round to the salary. It wasn't money.

DINKA: Who knows? You want this Kir?

ADAM: (*Consulting his file*) She wrote to me in reply to the ad, she said was fed up with working for the big boys, she wanted something more challenging and this job sounded like fun . . .

DINKA: Who knows? Who knows with those women? You're better off without her. I tell you. You get yourself a nice clean girl, eh?

ADAM: A nice clean girl?

DINKA: From a good house.

ADAM: She's not a – nice girl . . .

(DINKA *laughs hollowly.*)

No?

DINKA: She take all your money. What she give you? Diseases.

ADAM: Diseases?

DINKA: A whore is a whore is a whore is a whore, eh?

ADAM: A whore? She's a whore? A prostitute?

DINKA: She sit for hours. One glass of tonic water. No menu. I know straightaway. I say who you waiting for, she say a man, I say what man, she say I don't know, I know him when I see him, I say watch it or you're out in the gutter, OK? . . . She's a whore. We get them. Not often but we get them. Saturday night, we get them. Cold night. No underclothes.

ADAM: My God. I've been talking to the wrong woman . . .

DINKA: That's what I'm telling you. You want this other glass?

ADAM: No. Yes. Leave it there. Where's the one I'm supposed to meet?

DINKA: There's another whore?

ADAM: No, no . . . I'm supposed to be meeting this woman. A business meeting.

(MAUREEN *returns. She has her coat on.*)

MAUREEN: Excuse me. I left my handbag.

DINKA: (*Confidentially, to* ADAM) Look out, look out. She wants to
    bargain. She's come back to bargain. Be careful, eh?
ADAM: (*To* DINKA) Yes, alright, I . . . (*To* MAUREEN) Excuse me.
MAUREEN: (*Who has retrieved her bag*) Goodnight.
ADAM: Please. Just a minute. Please. (*Urgently*) Please! I say!
MAUREEN: (*Stopping and turning to him, reluctantly*) What?
    (DINKA *shakes his head disapprovingly and goes off muttering.*)
ADAM: I – er . . .
MAUREEN: (*Impatiently*) Yes?
ADAM: I apologize. There's been a misunderstanding . . .
MAUREEN: There certainly has. (*Threatening to leave*) Is that it?
ADAM: No. Just a second, I – I just wanted to explain. You see, I
    thought you were someone else – please, won't you have your
    drink . . . ?
MAUREEN: No, thank you.
ADAM: I realize, I wasted your time and – your time is – is money
    and I'm really sorry. You see I was looking for a –
MAUREEN: I know what you were looking for . . .
ADAM: I was expecting to interview an office manager –
MAUREEN: Dear God! Whatever next, she asked?
ADAM: A Miss Llewellyn who was supposed to meet me here.
MAUREEN: Do I look as if I was born at lunchtime?
ADAM: It's true. Absolutely true. Look! (*Thrusting his folder at
    her*) Look! Look. Please. Please.
    (*Something in his tone makes* MAUREEN *look at the folder for a
    second. She then studies him.*)
    The truth. Honestly.
MAUREEN: You're either a brilliant liar or you're an idiot.
ADAM: I'm – an idiot. Probably. Yes.
MAUREEN: Yes. I'm inclined to believe you.
ADAM: Thank you. (*Offering for her to sit*) Please. Will you finish
    your drink?
MAUREEN: Alright. Just the drink.
ADAM: If it's not taking up too much of your time . . .
MAUREEN: What else would I be doing?
    (*She sits.* ADAM *follows suit.*)
ADAM: Good health.
MAUREEN: Cheers!

(*They drink.*)

It's nice. I've never had this. What is it?

ADAM: Well. It's basically champagne.

MAUREEN: Champagne? Well. You know how to live, you office managers, don't you?

(*She smiles at him. He smiles back. Then frowns suddenly.*)

ADAM: You're so young.

MAUREEN: How do you mean?

ADAM: I'm sorry. To be – doing – what you're doing . . .

MAUREEN: Doing what?

ADAM: Oh, I've no right to lecture you – why don't I mind my own business? – it's your life – your choice, presumably . . .

MAUREEN: My what?

ADAM: You want to sell yourself for money to every man who asks you, that's up to you. It just seems to me that –

MAUREEN: You're doing it again, aren't you?

ADAM: What?

MAUREEN: (*Loudly, angrily rising*) Look, Clarence, for the forty-ninth time, I am not a tart, alright. I am not a prostitute, a call girl, a street-walker, a topless masseuse or a kinky French teacher. I don't do topless Lesbian dancing in mud, leather, rubber or bloody bri-nylon. So you'll have to get your rocks off elsewhere, alright? Now bugger off!

(ADAM *has risen in horror and is staring round the restaurant in alarm.*

DINKA *enters swiftly.*)

DINKA: (*To* MAUREEN) Alright. I warn you. Out now. Out. None of that in here. Out.

(DINKA *grasps* MAUREEN's *elbow.*)

MAUREEN: (*Wriggling free*) Get your hands off me! What's the matter with this place, you're all raving lunatics . . .

DINKA: Out! I call Mr Calvinu . . .

ADAM: Just a minute! You're not – You're not a – a prostitute . . .

MAUREEN: I've told you, no!

ADAM: What are you, then?

MAUREEN: I'm a fucking hairdresser, aren't I?

DINKA: (*Deeply shocked*) Hey! Hey! Hey! Hey! Hey! Now I get the manager.

ADAM: Just a minute! Just a minute!

MAUREEN: It's alright, don't bother, I'm off.

ADAM: Please, please! Wait a minute! (*To* DINKA) I will vouch for this lady –

MAUREEN: I don't need vouching for –

ADAM: For both of us. Please. I vouch for both of us. There's been a terrible misunderstanding . . .

MAUREEN: Another one?

ADAM: Yes.

MAUREEN: How many more goes do you get?

ADAM: No more. (*To* DINKA) It's alright. We're alright. Wait a second . . .

DINKA: (*As he goes, muttering*) How long you want me to wait? Till she's naked on the table . . . ?

(DINKA *goes off.*)

MAUREEN: (*Making to follow* DINKA) I've had a basin full of that one . . .

ADAM: I'm sorry. I don't know how all this happened.

MAUREEN: Well, I'm bloody sure I don't.

ADAM: Will you sit down again?

MAUREEN: What's the point? You're only going to ask me to pose for mucky pictures, I know you are.

ADAM: I'm not. I promise.

MAUREEN: Listen, I came here tonight because I was computer-dated, matched with a man called Robin who smokes a pipe and likes Stevie Wonder and Billy Joel. And he didn't sound like much, but he sounded better than nothing. So I put on my most boring clothes and I came out for a really boring evening. But at least I was going out somewhere because I couldn't stand another Saturday night at home without going raving mad. But I didn't come out for all this. God almighty!

ADAM: Oh, that's – I feel so awful about this. Look, we'll try and find this man of yours, shall we? Robin. He's probably sitting waiting here somewhere –

MAUREEN: What are you talking about? He'll have run a mile by now, won't he? With his Billy Joel under his arm and his pipe blazing . . . (*She digs out a card from her handbag.*) Look. (*She shows* ADAM.) Robin Diddswell – the Espresso . . .

ADAM: The Espresso?

MAUREEN: That's what it says.

ADAM: That's not this place . . . This is Essa de Calvi. The
    Espresso is further along.

MAUREEN: It is?

ADAM: About a hundred yards.

MAUREEN: I wondered why he hadn't reserved.

ADAM: The Espresso's a wine bar.

MAUREEN: A wine bar?

ADAM: Quite good soup. Sandwiches.

MAUREEN: Soup and sandwiches?

ADAM: Well, he may have been planning to go on from there . . .

MAUREEN: No. That doesn't sound like Robin somehow, does it?

ADAM: Would you – care to . . . Perhaps? With me?

MAUREEN: Well. (*She considers*) What about your friend?

ADAM: I think she's probably fled as well.

MAUREEN: Never know her luck. She may end up listening to
    Billy Joel . . .

ADAM: Choking to death on pipe smoke . . .

MAUREEN: Right.

    (*They smile at each other.*)

    In that case, yes. Thank you very much.

ADAM: Good.

    (*They sit.*)

MAUREEN: But we go dutch, alright?

ADAM: Well, we'll see. Whatever, it's clearly understood. Just the
    meal. Nothing else. No strings. No obligations. Right?

MAUREEN: Right. No strings . . .

    (*They smile at each other again as the lights fade on them and
    return to the main area. It is a few minutes later.* GERRY *rises.*
    LAURA *remains seated. She is dozing gently.*)

GERRY: Right. You ready for off?

LAURA: (*Starting awake*) What? What's the time?

GERRY: Just gone one.

    (*He starts to help gather up her presents, in particular her clock.*)

LAURA: I dozed off, I think.

GERRY: Soon be home.

LAURA: Now, you're positive you can drive?

87

GERRY: (*Lifting the clock*) I can drive . . . God, this is a weight.
LAURA: I said it was. Damn stupid thing to give anyone. Now, I
    don't want you falling asleep . . .
GERRY: I'm not going to fall asleep. Come on! Shift yourself . . .
LAURA: I need my coat . . .
    (*They start to leave.*)
    You got the cloakroom ticket?
GERRY: Yes. There's not a lot left in there, though. They
    shouldn't have trouble finding it.
LAURA: You still need the ticket . . .
GERRY: I've got the bloody ticket, I've just said I have,
    woman . . .
LAURA: (*Rather wearily*) Don't shout at me, Gerry, don't shout,
    there's no need to shout at me, is there . . . ?
    (*They have gone. The lights fade and come up again on* GLYN
    and STEPHANIE's *table. It is Tuesday, 16 November, almost
    two years now since the birthday dinner. For once,* GLYN *is the
    one seated alone. He appears to have all but finished his meal.
    He looks at his watch rather anxiously. He seems somehow
    flabbier both physically and mentally. He continues to sip his
    coffee.
    In a moment,* STEPHANIE *arrives. Her image has changed
    dramatically since we last saw her. She has slimmed right down
    and is thinner than we have ever seen her, almost gaunt. There is
    a new-found inner determination about her. Someone who's been
    through personal crisis and survived.
    She stands by the table.* GLYN *does not see her immediately.
    When he does look up he doesn't, at first, recognize her.*)
STEPHANIE: (*Smiling*) Hi . . .
    (GLYN *looks up and stares at her.*)
    Hallo, Glyn.
GLYN: Steph? Hallo. I thought for a minute you weren't –
STEPHANIE: Sorry. Things piled up. Have you got long?
GLYN: (*Nervously*) Well, I have to be . . . I have to be back by
    two, actually. I – Never mind, we have twenty minutes. Do
    you want to eat? Do you want to order? Waiter! I'm afraid, I
    have started. Well, as you can see I've finished, actually –
STEPHANIE: I don't want anything to eat . . .

GLYN: You won't?

STEPHANIE: I don't bother much with lunch these days. I'll have a glass of water . . .

GLYN: Waiter! You ought to eat lunch, you know . . .

STEPHANIE: I find I don't need it.

GLYN: Well, you look – great. You look really good.

STEPHANIE: Thank you. Lost a bit of weight. How are you?

GLYN: Oh, I'm fine. (*Calling*) Waiter! (*To her*) I'm still with Barry. Helping Barry out. He needed a hand. It's good. It's a good feeling. Getting shot of all that responsibility. At least temporarily. Working for somebody else. Let them worry about it, eh? For a change?

STEPHANIE: (*Smiling*) Yes.

GLYN: So. Back on the road. Never thought I'd do that again. That's how I started for Dad, you know. Trudging the streets with a sample case. Well, trudging the streets in a company car . . .

(*He laughs. He is very nervous and unsure. She smiles.*)

STEPHANIE: (*Calling*) Waiter!

(TUTO *arrives like a shot.*)

TUTO: Madametta? What can I – ? (*Recognizing* STEPHANIE) Madama! It's you!

STEPHANIE: Yes.

TUTO: Fantastical. You look fantastical. Does she not look fantastical?

GLYN: Yes, indeed. I was –

TUTO: (*Approvingly*) Mmm! Mmm! Like a fashion model. You light up the restaurant.

STEPHANIE: (*Only slightly embarrassed*) Thank you.

TUTO: It's a long time. One year. No?

STEPHANIE: Nearly that . . .

TUTO: What can I get you? Some menus? Maybe the sweet trolley, eh?

STEPHANIE: (*Smiling*) No, not the sweet trolley.

TUTO: No sweet trolley?

STEPHANIE: No. Just a bottle of water, please. Still water.

TUTO: Just a water. Seerar?

GLYN: Yes, I'll have another coffee. Black . . .

TUTO: Straightaway . . .

    (TUTO *goes off.*)

STEPHANIE: This place is as busy as ever.

GLYN: Yes. It's had its ups and downs but –

STEPHANIE: I haven't been in here for ages. Must be a year.
    Nothing's changed. I don't think it's even been repainted.

GLYN: Well, old man Calvinu's been laid up recently . . .

STEPHANIE: Oh, dear. Serious?

GLYN: Heart, I think. He's taking it easier. He isn't quite so
    much in evidence these days. What's all that about the sweet
    trolley . . . ?

STEPHANIE: Nothing. Private joke.

GLYN: Oh.

    (TUTO *returns with a bottle of water and a glass on the tray.*)

TUTO: (*Setting this down by* STEPHANIE) 'Scoos. One water.

STEPHANIE: No, I'm sorry, that's fizzy water. I asked for still
    water.

TUTO: Sorry?

STEPHANIE: I asked for still water. Not fizzy. I don't want this.

TUTO: Sorry. Madama. A million pardons. Still water, of course.
    (*He whisks the bottle and glass away.*) 'Scoos. Five seconds.
    Coffee is coming.

    (TUTO *goes off again.*)

GLYN: So. You've – You've met someone?

STEPHANIE: Yes. I've met someone.

GLYN: Good, good. Serious? I mean is it . . . ?

STEPHANIE: I hope it is. I've agreed to move in with him. With
    the kids. He's divorced, on his own. No children. So . . .

GLYN: What does he do?

STEPHANIE: He's a surgeon. An orthopaedic surgeon.

GLYN: (*Impressed*) Oh . . .

STEPHANIE: This is why I wanted to meet really. We could have
    done it all by letter but –

    (TUTO *arrives again, this time with a bottle of still water and a
    glass on a tray.*)

TUTO: Madama. Still water.

STEPHANIE: Thank you.

TUTO: Coffee's just coming . . .

(TUTO *goes off again.*)

STEPHANIE: Listen, I know you haven't got much time, so – The
point is, I think I would like a divorce. I know you've always
said, let's not make irreversible decisions, let's leave things
unresolved just in case we decide to . . . Well, let's be honest,
it's not going to happen is it, Glyn –

GLYN: I don't know, it –

STEPHANIE: Well, it isn't. Not from my side. Not now. It's too
late. We've moved on. We both have. All I'm saying is, let's
tidy things up, shall we? I think – I probably will remarry –
sooner or later – For the kids. No, not just for the kids but –
And then there's you and Sarah, isn't there? How does she
feel about this arrangement? Dragging on? I'm sure she'd
like it tidied up, wouldn't she? I can't believe she wouldn't
. . . Surely?

(*A pause.*)

So? What do you say? It makes sense, doesn't it?

(GLYN *does not reply.*)

Glyn? It does, doesn't it? Really? Yes?

(GLYN *nods.*)

OK. Well. That's all I came to say, really. (*Looking at her
watch*) I ought to – I ought to get on . . . (*Gently*) It's best.
Honestly, it is.

GLYN: Would you – would you do something for me?

STEPHANIE: What?

GLYN: Could you – write to my mother – I'm not suggesting you
go and see her – just write and say that you're the one who
asked for the divorce. Not me.

STEPHANIE: You want me to write and tell her that?

GLYN: Would you mind?

STEPHANIE: I don't mind. OK.

GLYN: She might believe it if you – You see before Dad died I
made him a promise that, for Mother's sake, I wouldn't, you
know, I wouldn't – walk out on you all, you know . . . I mean
I know I haven't been actually living with you, but I haven't
walked out on you, have I? Not technically. I've still been
looking after you. From a distance. If you appreciate the
distinction.

91

STEPHANIE: Your mother may live in a world of her own these days, but I think she might have seen through that, Glyn . . .

GLYN: Please, you will write to her, won't you?

STEPHANIE: I've said I will.

GLYN: And if you ever feel you can face her for half an hour, she'd love to see the kids again. She really would . . .

STEPHANIE: Oh, Glyn . . .

GLYN: It'd mean so much to her, you know . . .

STEPHANIE: She doesn't want to see them, Glyn. She's not even interested in them.

GLYN: Oh, she is, she –

STEPHANIE: The only thing that interests her is her. Her and all those bloody dogs she keeps adopting. How many has she got now, five isn't it?

GLYN: Six.

STEPHANIE: Six. For God's sake. She's turned that house into a kennels.

GLYN: She'd still love to see Tim and Jess . . .

STEPHANIE: Glyn, get it through your head – she doesn't care about you or me – or Sarah or the kids . . . She is not interested. She is a selfish, self-centred, destructive old woman and she's not worth ruining your life for. Forget about us two, you and me, we're history. Start again, live your own life and to hell with her – marry Sarah, have fifteen kids. Your mother's not worth it. She doesn't love you. She doesn't love anybody except herself, alright?

GLYN: She loves Adam.

STEPHANIE: I even doubt that, you know.

GLYN: Oh, no. She loves Adam. She may not love me. I know she doesn't. But she loves Adam.

STEPHANIE: You know what I heard the other day? I was in the hairdressers. My regular one was off sick and guess who I got instead? Maureen. Remember, that girl of Adam's he was so keen on? And, do you know what she told me? Why Adam stopped seeing her? Apparently your mother told him that Maureen's behaviour on her birthday evening upset his father so deeply, that was the reason he got drunk and drove off the road.

92

GLYN: I don't believe it. Mother would never have said that.

STEPHANIE: Maybe not, I don't know. Anyway, Maureen's alright. Flashing a brand new engagement ring with a diamond the size of a dinner plate. Listen, what's going to happen to Adam? Is he ever going to move out of there? Live on his own again?

GLYN: I don't know. I imagine so. I've no idea what he plans to do.

STEPHANIE: Well, I've lost touch. He used to ring me but – If you do see him, tell him my advice is to get out from under. I must dash. I don't know where they've gone with your coffee. (*As she rises*) See you soon. I'll keep in touch.
(*She kisses him, perfunctorily. He remains seated.*)

GLYN: You know – just before you came, I was sitting here and it occurred to me . . . You remember that night – the last night we were all together as a family – the night before Dad was killed . . . ?

STEPHANIE: Yes, it was that same evening. Mother's birthday party . . .

GLYN: And you and I, we were all set to start again – and Adam had his new girl and Mum and Dad looked so happy and – well, the point is – I doubt if any of us knew it at the time – it was something Dad said, actually – that was probably one of the best, the happiest moments of our lives. Only the trouble with those sorts of moments is that you seldom ever realize what they are – until they've gone. Do you see? I mean very rarely do you find yourself saying to yourself, I am happy *now*. Sometimes you say, I was happy *then*. Or sometimes even, I will be happy *when* . . . But rarely do you get to realize it *now*. If you know what I mean.

STEPHANIE: (*Gently*) It's for the best, Glyn. It really is. Promise. You'll see. Bye, then.

GLYN: (*Sadly*) Bye.
(STEPHANIE *hesitates for a second about leaving him and then hurries away.* GLYN *remains where he is.*
ADAM, *dressed as a waiter, enters with a cup of black coffee on a tray.*)

ADAM: Did someone order a black coffee?

GLYN: Yes, it's a bit late now, though, I'm – (*Recognizing* ADAM)
Oh. Hallo.

ADAM: Hi.

GLYN: What are you doing?

ADAM: I'm working here.

GLYN: Since when?

ADAM: Since yesterday.

GLYN: As a waiter?

ADAM: Yes. Mum had a word with old man Calvinu. He said he'd
give me a try. It's only temporary, you know. While I get
things sorted out. I'm going to night school as well . . .

GLYN: Oh yes? Architecture? Right?

ADAM: No, bass guitar . . .

GLYN: Ah.

ADAM: You want this coffee?

GLYN: It's too late now, I have to go. You were a hell of a time.

ADAM: I know. I have trouble working the machine. It's only my
second day.

GLYN: Yes.

ADAM: Do you want it then? Only I can't take it back.

GLYN: No, I don't want it.

ADAM: You'll have to pay for it.

GLYN: I'm not paying for it, I don't want it.

ADAM: Oh.

(GLYN *gets up*.)
How's Sarah?

GLYN: Who?

ADAM: Sarah? I presume that was Sarah who left?

GLYN: No. That was Stephanie.

ADAM: Steph! I didn't recognize her. How is she?

GLYN: She's – well.

ADAM: I haven't talked to her for ages. Well, I don't get much
chance these days. Soon as I get home, there's all Mother's
dogs to feed, take for walks . . . All go, eh?

GLYN: (*Smiling, feebly*) Yes.

ADAM: Are you – are you thinking of getting together with Steph
again, then?

GLYN: No.

94

ADAM: Ah. Sticking with Sarah?

GLYN: No, I'm not with Sarah, either.

ADAM: Oh. What happened?

GLYN: What usually happens, Adam. She went her way, I went mine . . .

ADAM: Yes. That's what usually happens. Except for Mum and Dad. They stuck it out.

GLYN: Yes, well. They were exceptional, weren't they? (*Making to leave*) Look, you drink that. I have to go.

ADAM: You want your bill?

GLYN: I'll get it at the desk. See you around.

ADAM: Yes. Sure.

(GLYN *goes off.* ADAM *has picked up the still full coffee cup and stands uncertainly with it.*)

Anyone want a coffee? Black coffee, going spare. Anyone want a coffee . . . ?

(*The lights cross to the main table. We are back to the night of the party, at the very start of the evening.* CALVINU *leads* GERRY *and* LAURA *into the room.*)

CALVINU: . . . through here, please. Tonight we have put you through here . . .

GERRY: This is all for us, is it?

CALVINU: Oh yes, all for you. It's suitable?

GERRY: Oh, it's fine. . .

LAURA: Yes, we've been in here before. For Adam's twenty-first . . .

CALVINU: For the twenty-first, I remember. And tonight it is your birthday, Laura. I wish you many, many happy returns of the day.

LAURA: Thank you.

CALVINU: I must apologize, I will be a little absent for some of the evening. We have a big, big party upstairs – they won't disturb you. If I may, I will join you later to drink your health, Laura. I will leave you in the hands of Tuto, you know him, he's my head waiter, he's very, very good . . .

GERRY: Yes, of course we know Tuto . . .

CALVINU: Everything you want, ask him please. Meanwhile I will see your guests are shown through and I will send through

95

the cocktails. Have a happy evening and a successful birthday party, OK?

LAURA: Thank you.

GERRY: Thank you, Ernesto.

(CALVINU *goes off*. GERRY *waits restlessly whilst* LAURA *inspects the table and the place settings*.)

LAURA: They've put you at this end, is that alright?

GERRY: Fine.

LAURA: You wouldn't prefer that other end?

GERRY: Makes no difference to me.

LAURA: I could swap you round. Put you at that other end.

GERRY: No, don't bother . . .

LAURA: It's no bother.

GERRY: I'm perfectly happy at that end. Leave it alone.

(*Pause*.)

LAURA: Sometimes you like to face the window, that's all.

GERRY: There's no point in facing the window, is there? It's pitch dark and the curtains are drawn.

LAURA: Suit yourself.

(*Pause*.)

GERRY: Do you want to?

LAURA: What?

GERRY: Swap round. Go that end?

LAURA: No. I don't want to swap ends. Why should I want to swap ends? Makes no difference to me where I sit. (*Studying the table again*) I've put that girl next to you here.

GERRY: What girl?

LAURA: Adam's girl – (*Straining to read the card*) Maureen, that's her name. Doesn't sound so promising, does it?

GERRY: We're reserving judgement now, aren't we?

LAURA: Yes . . . Well, I hope Stephanie's got a new line in conversation, that's all I can say. If she talks babies all evening, I'll throttle her –

GERRY: Come on, it's your birthday. Don't get off on the wrong foot . . .

LAURA: It's alright for you –

GERRY: She thinks you're interested.

LAURA: Why should I be interested . . .

96

GERRY: You're Timmy's grandmother, they're very proud of him. They think you'll be proud of him, too . . . It's sort of natural, you know.

LAURA: I still don't see why we should have to talk about him all evening. God, she's a boring girl, isn't she? What a bore? Only someone like Glyn could put up with her . . .

GERRY: (*Loudly*) Ah! Here they are . . .

(STEPHANIE *comes in, as at the start of the play. She carries a small gift-wrapped parcel – the earrings*).

STEPHANIE: Hallo!

LAURA: Hallo! Come in . . .

(*They kiss.*)

STEPHANIE: Happy birthday, then.

LAURA: Thank you.

STEPHANIE: Here you are. Little something.

LAURA: Oh, bless you. You shouldn't . . .

STEPHANIE: Glyn's got something for you as well. A bigger something. He's just dealing with the coats. (*Moving to* GERRY) Hallo, Gerry . . .

(*They kiss.*)

GERRY: Hallo, Steph. How are you? How's Timmy, then?

STEPHANIE: Oh, he's well. He's bonny. I brought you the new pictures. Just had them developed.

GERRY: Oh, grand . . .

LAURA: Lovely.

GERRY: You look good.

STEPHANIE: Well. I feel good. I feel much better.

GERRY: Yes. We're both . . . you know . . . thrilled you're . . .

(*Before he can continue,* GLYN *enters boisterously. He carries a large wrapped gift – the clock*).

GLYN: Hallo, hallo. Are we in here tonight, are we?

LAURA: Yes, they've got a do upstairs apparently. Hallo, dear.

GLYN: Hallo, Mum.

(*He kisses her proffered cheek.*)

Happy birthday. Here. Something for you. Look out, it's a bit of a weight.

LAURA: (*Trying to take it*) Oh, Glyn, it's terribly heavy. I can't possibly hold that, don't be so silly. Put it on the table.

97

GLYN: (*Doing so*) I think you'll like it. (*To* STEPHANIE) I think
she'll like it, don't you?

STEPHANIE: She'll love it. It's brilliant. He picked it all by himself.
I had nothing to do with it.

LAURA: Where's Adam? I hope he's not going to be late as usual.

STEPHANIE: Is he bringing his new girl?

LAURA: Yes, whatsername . . .

GERRY: Maureen.

LAURA: Maureen. She's a hairdresser, apparently.

STEPHANIE: Oh, right. Useful. Must give her a try, mustn't we?

GERRY: Where's the bloke with those cocktails? I asked them to
bring them through. Cocktails the minute we arrive, I said.

GLYN: Want me to check?

GERRY: No, it's alright I'll – (*Seeing more guests*) Ah. Come in,
come in . . .

LAURA: Oh, here they are.

(ADAM *enters with* MAUREEN, *dressed as at the start of the play*.)

ADAM: Hallo.

STEPHANIE: Hallo.

GLYN: Hallo.

MAUREEN: (*Shyly*) Hallo.

ADAM: Everyone, this is – this is Maureen. My friend Maureen.
Maureen, this is my mother, Laura.

LAURA: (*With great charm*) Hallo, Maureen.

MAUREEN: Hallo.

ADAM: This is my father . . .

GERRY: Hallo, Maureen, I'm Gerry . . .

MAUREEN: How do you do . . .

ADAM: My brother, Glyn . . .

GLYN: Hallo.

MAUREEN: Hallo.

ADAM: And last but not least, this is my sister-in-law,
Stephanie . . .

STEPHANIE: Hallo, Maureen, good to meet you . . .

MAUREEN: Nice to meet you. Thank you.

(*A brief silence. They all look at* MAUREEN *but no one speaks.*
MAUREEN *is aware she is somewhat overdressed. She smiles as
best she can.*)

GERRY: Well. All met. Shall we all sit down? I think we've got our places marked for us, haven't we? Maureen, I'm afraid you're stuck this end next to me.

MAUREEN: Right. Thank you.

(TUTO *enters with a tray of champagne cocktails.*)

GERRY: And, Steph, you're the other side of me here . . . Ah, Tuto, at last. Where have you been, feller?

TUTO: I'm sorry, I'm sorry. With the champagne, it's not good to open to the last minute. (*To* LAURA) Madama, a cocktail?

LAURA: Thank you, I'm gasping for something.

GERRY: (*Under this last, to* MAUREEN) I could open a bottle of champagne a damn sight quicker than this lot . . .

(MAUREEN *laughs.*)

TUTO: (*Continuing, uninterrupted*) Madama, happy birthday.

LAURA: Thank you.

TUTO: (*To* ADAM) Seerar?

ADAM: (*Accepting his drink*) Thank you.

STEPHANIE: (*As* TUTO *continues round the table, to* MAUREEN) Did you come by taxi?

MAUREEN: No, we walked.

TUTO: (*Giving a glass to* STEPHANIE) Madama . . .

STEPHANIE: (*To* TUTO) Thank you. (*To* MAUREEN) Walked? That's noble.

MAUREEN: I don't live too far away.

GERRY: Whereabouts do you live?

TUTO: (*To* GERRY) Mister Stratton.

GERRY: Thank you.

MAUREEN: Harwick Road. It's just off North . . .

TUTO: (*To* MAUREEN) Madametta?

MAUREEN: Thank you.

GERRY: Oh yes, we know Harwick Road . . .

LAURA: Oh, yes. Don't we have warehouses somewhere round there?

TUTO: (*Serving* GLYN *last*) Seerar.

GLYN: Thank you.

GERRY: Yes, we do . . . We have our paint store down there . . .

ADAM: Maureen lives the other end. By the canal.

LAURA: Oh, in one of those lovely little cottages?

MAUREEN: Yes.

LAURA: By the canal?

MAUREEN: Yes.

LAURA: Lovely old places. Aren't they damp, at all?

MAUREEN: No, not really, no.

LAURA: Amazing. I'd have thought being that near water. (*To* STEPHANIE) I don't think I could live near canals. I'd be frightened of rats and things, wouldn't you?

STEPHANIE: Well . . .

MAUREEN: We don't have rats . . .

ADAM: They don't have rats, Mother . . .

LAURA: Oh really. I thought that's where rats lived. Near canals . . .

ADAM: Mother . . .

MAUREEN: They can live anywhere. Can rats.

LAURA: Really?

MAUREEN: Wherever there's dirt. Or filth. Or any sort of shit for that matter.

(*A brief pause.*)

GERRY: (*Smoothing things over*) Well, I think a little toast is in order. I don't want to make a long speech but . . . Just to say, happy birthday to Laura. And to thank her for putting up with me for another year . . . And here's to many more of those. I'd just like to add, it's very nice to see us all together as family – Glyn and Steph – and Adam – and to welcome Maureen. I hope we'll be seeing a lot more of you, Maureen.

STEPHANIE: (*Kindly*) Hear! Hear!

(MAUREEN *gives her a smile of gratitude.*)

GERRY: And without getting philosophic – which as you know isn't my way –

(LAURA *gives a short ironic laugh.*)

Nevertheless – you know, in life, you get moments – just occasionally which you can positively identify as being among the happy moments. They come up occasionally, even take you by surprise, and sometimes you're so busy worrying about tomorrow or thinking about yesterday that you tend to miss out on them altogether. I'd like to hope tonight might be one such moment. And if it is – let's not

miss out on this one, alright? All that really means is, enjoy
yourselves. (*Slight pause*) Anyway. To Laura and – to happy
times.

(*They all rise, except for* LAURA, *and raise their glasses.*)

ALL (*Except* LAURA): To Laura . . . happy times . . .

LAURA: (*Still seated, murmuring*) Happy times . . .

(*They drink.* MAUREEN *alone remains standing after they are
seated, draining her glass.*)

MAUREEN: (*Banging down her glass rather noisily*) Lovely.

(*She smiles at them all. Realizes she is the only one still standing
and sits. As she does so, the lights fade to a blackout.*)